The Unreasonable
Virtue of Fly Fishing

Nonfiction

Salmon: A Fish, the Earth, and the History of Their Common Fate

Milk!: A 10,000-Year Food Fracas

Havana: A Subtropical Delirium

Paper: Paging Through History

*International Night: A Father and Daughter Cook Their
Way Around the World*

*Ready for a Brand New Beat: How "Dancing in the Street"
Became the Anthem for a Changing America*

Birdseye: The Adventures of a Curious Man

Hank Greenberg: The Hero Who Didn't Want to Be One

*What? Are These the 20 Most Important Questions in
Human History—or Is This a Game of 20 Questions?*

*The Eastern Stars: How Baseball Changed the
Dominican Town of San Pedro de Macoris*

*The Food of a Younger Land: A Portrait of American
Food from the Lost WPA Files*

*The Last Fish Tale: The Fate of the Atlantic and Survival in
Gloucester, America's Oldest Fishing Port and Most Original Town*

The Big Oyster: History on the Half Shell

Nonviolence: A History of a Dangerous Idea

1968: The Year That Rocked the World

*Choice Cuts: A Savory Selection of Food Writing from
Around the World and Throughout History*

Salt: A World History

The Basque History of the World

Cod: A Biography of the Fish That Changed the World

A Chosen Few: The Resurrection of European Jewry

A Continent of Islands: Searching for the Caribbean Destiny

Fiction

City Beasts: Fourteen Stories of Uninvited Wildlife

Edible Stories: A Novel in Sixteen Parts

*"The Belly of Paris" by Émile Zola: A New Translation with
an Introduction by Mark Kurlansky*

Boogaloo on 2nd Avenue: A Novel of Pastry, Guilt, and Music

The White Man in the Tree and Other Stories

Children/Young Adult

*Frozen in Time: Clarence Birdseye's Outrageous
Idea About Frozen Food*

Battle Fatigue

World Without Fish

The Story of Salt

The Girl Who Swam to Euskadi

The Cod's Tale

The Unreasonable
Virtue of Fly Fishing

Mark Kurlansky

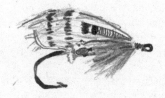

BLOOMSBURY PUBLISHING
NEW YORK · LONDON · OXFORD · NEW DELHI · SYDNEY

BLOOMSBURY PUBLISHING
Bloomsbury Publishing Inc.
1385 Broadway, New York, NY 10018, USA

BLOOMSBURY, BLOOMSBURY PUBLISHING, and the Diana logo
are trademarks of Bloomsbury Publishing Plc

First published in the United States 2021
This edition published 2022

ISBN: HB: 978-1-63557-307-7; PB: 978-1-63557-875-1;
EBOOK: 978-1-63557-308-4

LIBRARY OF CONGRESS CATALOGING-IN-PUBLICATION DATA IS AVAILABLE

2 4 6 8 10 9 7 5 3 1

Typeset by Westchester Publishing Services
Printed and bound in the U.S.A.

To find out more about our authors and books visit
www.bloomsbury.com and sign up for our newsletters.

Bloomsbury books may be purchased for business or promotional use.
For information on bulk purchases please contact Macmillan Corporate and
Premium Sales Department at specialmarkets@macmillan.com.

To Talia Feiga, my fishing buddy

*My father was very sure about certain matters pertaining
to the universe. To him all good things—trout as well
as eternal salvation—come by grace and grace comes
by art and art does not come easy.*

—NORMAN MACLEAN, *A RIVER RUNS THROUGH IT*

There's no one more silly than a fisherman.

—MEGAN BOYD, RENOWNED SCOTTISH FLY-TIER

CONTENTS

Winter Without Tolstoy on the Big Wood River

He was fond of angling, and seemed proud of being able to like such a stupid occupation.

—LEO TOLSTOY, *ANNA KARENINA*

Stepping into the Big Wood River on a winter day, I feel the current wrap around my legs like the embrace of an old friend. That an icy river can have a warm embrace is one of nature's ironies.

Ernest Hemingway fished the Big Wood River and even chose its bank as the place to die. He understood. Tolstoy, who understood so much about human nature, just didn't understand, or at least he created a character who didn't.

In *Anna Karenina*, he wrote of two brothers who were wealthy landowners. To the first brother, there was nothing better than working in the fields. He could not understand why the other wanted to go off and fish for perch. At the end of the day, he would meet up with the second brother and be mystified at how happy that brother was after fishing all day even though he hadn't caught a single fish.

It is not an uncommon divide: the one who fishes versus the one who doesn't. The one who does can never explain the urge to the one who doesn't.

Every winter in central Idaho while the smart set is gliding down the mountains of Sun Valley experiencing their own version of exhilaration, I make my way down snowy banks into the freezing Big Wood River in the hopes that a large and handsome rainbow trout will pull on my fly. There are days when I catch a dozen fish and days when I catch none, but I always return to town filled with the sense of peace that comes after having had a great day. If I catch no fish, if my fingers are so cold that they have turned bright red and no longer work— no matter. Any day spent fishing on a wintry river is a great day. How is it possible that someone who could write *Anna Karenina* couldn't see that?

IT WAS MY interest in the Basques that first brought me to central Idaho, to the town of Ketchum. Earlier in my career, I had written a book about the Basques and spent much time in their homeland, which in their language is called Euskal Herria, in northern Spain and southwestern France. The Basques herd sheep on their farms, which is what had brought *them* to central Idaho a century before I arrived.

The practice of bringing outsiders into the rugged, remote mountains near Ketchum to herd sheep had begun in the nineteenth century, when local sheep producers brought in Scots, because, due to the expansion of the cattle industry, there were not enough shepherds to tend to the area's huge flocks. The sheep industry was replacing mining in central Idaho. Scots knew something about tending sheep, but soon they assimilated and educated their children, who became economically successful in other fields or moved back to a newly industrialized Scotland. At this same time, in the beginning of the twentieth century, Basque farms in Europe, especially on the French side, were in crisis, and so the Idaho community was able to lure Basque farmers, who also knew something about sheep—housing the farmers in a building in Greenwich Village in New York until a suitable flock for them to tend could be found and they were placed on westbound trains. The Basques then went the way of the Scots, building a large, successful community in central Idaho, and in the late twentieth century the Peruvians were brought in.

Because of my Basque connection, I was asked to speak at the sheep festival held every fall in Ketchum. My wife and daughter came with me, and all three of us were immediately taken by the area's semi-wilderness. We decided to return in the winter for some world-class skiing, oddly forgetting that we were not world-class skiers. I liked cross-country, and had skied a few mountains in far tamer Vermont, but was not fond of riding a chair or gondola to a mountaintop, rushing down, and riding back up again. It seemed to me that the greatest moment in skiing was when you finally got to take off your boots.

I skied a little during our first winter in Idaho, but then I was told that there is winter fly fishing on the Big Wood River and that was the end of my skiing. My wife, Marian, continued to ski and my daughter, Talia, skied some days and fished others and was remarkably good at both. I have tried to get back to fish the Big Wood every winter since.

THE BIG WOOD begins at the Galena Summit, about 8,700 feet above sea level, formed from churning streams descending the rugged and aptly named Sawtooth Mountains, whose rough-cut, sharp-pointed, snow-covered white peaks line up in a row like a lower jaw of wolf teeth. There, the angry waters join together and then split off into the Salmon River and the Big Wood River at what is surely one of the most beautiful spots on earth.

The Salmon River carves a 425-mile canyon that in places is deeper than the Grand Canyon. Its steep banks of rough rock, at times almost vertical, are covered with bright chartreuse and yellow lichen, while dark, clear water rushes and churns below. Lewis and Clark dubbed the Salmon "the River of No Return," because its current was so strong that they could not paddle back up it. But the Nez Perce, in whose territory the river ran, knew well how to paddle upstream. They were skilled salmon fishermen who lived off the river's rich salmon runs. Later, they also learned to be fine horsemen and deadly riflemen, and they were the last native tribe to be defeated by the U.S. Army. Their last chief on the Salmon River, White Bird, never surrendered nor was captured, but fled to safety in Canada.

I love to fish the Salmon, but it is not open in the winter. The Big Wood is open to fish trout, though only for catch-and-release fishing.

After separating from the Salmon, the Big Wood chortles and snarls for 137 miles, descending the Boulder Mountains in Sawtooth country down to where the riverbanks are low and the casting is easy, just past the town of Ketchum. Along the way, other tributaries join it, including the Warm Springs Creek, whose junction with the Big Wood is an excellent spot to catch trout. Past Ketchum, the Big Wood merges with the Little Wood and becomes the Malad River, which flows into the Snake River and then, like all Idaho rivers, leaves the state to flow into the Columbia River and finally the Pacific.

The Big Wood is not the easiest river to wade into, especially in the winter. The current is strong and the river bottom is covered with large slippery rocks, which makes it easy to lose your balance and fall. I have never fallen in, but if I did, my fishing day would be over. I would have to get out of my wet clothes and go somewhere warm. The river has deep quiet pools, drifting at the edge of the fast current, where the rainbow trout like to relax and grab food, including fishers' flies.

Which leads to the only two rules of fly fishing that cannot be broken: you cannot fall in and you must keep your fly in the water as much as possible. Everything else depends on circumstance.

Rainbow trout are remarkably designed. In the river only their dark backs can be seen, so well camouflaged that you rarely notice them until you hook one. But once the fish is pulled from the water, it is stunning, an almost iridescent rainbow of hot pastel colors.

Big Wood trout are called "cut bows." They have the rainbow trout's typical brilliant colors on their sides, but sometimes also sport a bright red slash of color at their throats. The red slash is the mark of another species of trout of the same genus, the cutthroat, which is abundant in the neighboring Snake River. This means that in the Big Wood, the cutthroats have somehow mixed with the rainbows.

The Big Wood is not stocked by a hatchery—which is significant because hatchery fish are a bit dumb. They don't have the survival skills of wild fish, which has led some to question the value of stocking rivers. Big Wood fish are wild and have the wisdom of experience, as in the summertime they face a constant swarm of catch-and-release fisherfolk who have seen the Robert Redford film *A River Runs Through It*. In 1925 Hemingway wrote to F. Scott Fitzgerald from Spain and defined his idea of heaven. One of his requirements was a trout stream that no one else is allowed to fish in. Fishing the Big Wood in winter is not quite that, but on a cold enough day it comes close. That's why I like winter fishing. I have the river to myself—and I have to contend with savvier fish. After running the gauntlet of the summer anglers, the fish know quite a bit about artificial flies and those strange creatures standing in the river holding poles. Fish learn.

One factor that makes hatchery fish easier to catch than wild ones is that they are used to being fed regularly and so will eat at any time. A wild trout is a different matter. Scientists tell us that trout like to feed when the temperature is between 50 and 68 degrees. It gets colder than that in the Big Wood, and as the temperature drops, a fish's metabolism slows down and it needs less food. You can still catch fish, though, because they have to eat eventually. I have fished the Big Wood when it was so cold that I struggled to keep my line from freezing and yet the trout kept biting. When the water is cold but the temperature is rising, as is often the case in the late winter, it is prime time for trout to eat. Trout will not eat or breed when the temperature gets above 68 degrees, however. In fact, they will die, partly because the warm water does not have

The Big Wood River, Idaho, in winter

enough oxygen. One of the biggest threats to trout is climate change.

Most of the time, but not always, the Big Wood can feel like a wild frontier. Hawks are hunting overhead. Merganser ducks with pointed narrow beaks, not the usual duckbills, fly in patrols over the river looking for small young fish. Beavers fell large cottonwood trees, patiently nibbling cone shapes at their bases until the points are thin enough for the trees to fall over. Often the beavers will chew down two or three large cottonwoods before they start eating the trees' black bark. Whole beaver families feast on the river's trees until there is nothing left along its shores except white poles. This changes the course of the river, creating fast, rushing, narrow streams and protected quiet pools that are good spots for fishing.

Hemingway, and many others, have claimed that central Idaho is at its best in the fall. The leaves on the aspen turn bright yellow—more than yellow. They cluster together in a golden glow, fall off, and butter the surface of the Big Wood. Between the clusters of aspen are red maple, turned a bright crimson.

These gold and red banks are beautiful, but for me the best time in central Idaho is when the jagged rocks, and the gray-blue sagebrush, and tumbleweed growing high on the slopes are covered with sparkling snow. In the rugged northern Rockies, there is a baldness to the mountains in winter. Even in the center of Ketchum there are hills too steep and rocky to build on.

One of the pleasures of winter fishing is that there is little food in the snowy high country and so its residents come down to the rivers to eat. Elk stop along the slopes to watch me fish and descend farther when I am gone. I find their cloven footprints along the riverbank. Sometimes a moose saunters down, looking for the first willow buds of spring. It is a little disconcerting to find an animal standing next to you that is a head taller than you and weighs well over a thousand pounds. But moose are not usually aggressive. I just try not to make them mad.

In the 1990s wolves, once commonplace here and then nearly extinct, were reintroduced to central Idaho. Cattle and sheep ranchers were upset, but the wolves fit in well, as they were part of the area's natural order. Hunters today complain that because of the wolves, there are fewer elk and deer to shoot, but there is little evidence of that. The animals are just more dispersed.

Attracting hunters is profitable business in central Idaho, which is why the wolves were nearly exterminated in the first place. That move led to the growth of unnaturally large ungulate populations in the Northern Rockies, making it easy for hunters to find and shoot their prey. Now they may have to do some stalking, as in older times.

There are wolves along the Big Wood, but they are too smart and agile to let themselves be seen. Brian Richter, my fishing guide for so long that he really seems to be more of a friend, has seen them. Brian is a lean westerner, a hunter and fisher who is so knowledgeable about his native Big Wood River Valley that he seems almost as much a part of nature there as the beaver or elk. When he catches a particularly beautiful fish, or when I do, he takes a picture and later paints a portrait.

When I first started to fish the Big Wood in 2006, there were a number of forest fires, and the rocks at the bottom of the river became black. I became accustomed to fishing in a black-rock river. But today the water is clear and the rocks have lost their black shrouds. They have returned to their natural green, orange, and yellow and the rainbow trout blend in, their spectacular colors—central electric cotton-candy-pink stripes surrounded by purple and orange stripes—matching the river bottom.

I fish in the late winter, when it is usually not so cold that the line starts freezing to the guide rings. Most of the river is no longer frozen by then, and there is already enough melt from the mountains to move its waters along quickly. Occasionally there might be a light snow flurry, with flakes landing as gentle as kisses on a baby, and the drifting flakes above the river remind me of the wonder I felt at first snowfalls in New England as a child.

You can dress warmly enough for everything but your fingers. Fly fishing is just too delicate for gloves, even fingerless ones. You need to be able to feel the line.

The Big Wood flows through the town of Ketchum. When Hemingway first discovered this town, it was a frontier outpost where rough men drank in downtown bars. The town had a population of just over 3,000 then, but of late has shrunk to less than that, and with more affluent people from the West Coast and fewer rough folk from the mountains.

When Hemingway bought his house on the Big Wood, it stood alone, in such a deserted spot that he could blow off his head with a shotgun behind his house without anyone seeing him. Were he still alive today, he would move, because now there are houses all around his. Ironically these newcomers are protective of their privacy. They try to chase away those who fish in front of their houses, which they have no right to do. No one owns the river.

People with money build houses on the river because they love it. But there are few things more destructive to a river, especially a fly fishing river, than houses along its banks. Building destroys the insect habitat, and insects are essential to a fish's survival.

Stone flies and small black midges are among the most common insects found along the Big Wood, and artificial flies made to resemble them are the ones I use most when fishing there. The stone fly is one of the oldest fly fish patterns we know of. It was described in the 1486 English book *Treatyse of Fysshynge wyth an Angle*, which recommended wrapping the fly's body in black wool with a touch of yellow wool under the wings, and using drake feathers for its tail and wings. Today's stone flies, made of woven black and brown feathers, resemble the actual long, slender insects much more than the fifteenth-century one did.

Stone flies, known to science as *plecopteran*, are found almost everywhere in the world except Antarctica. A female lays up to a thousand eggs, dropping them in running water or on rocks or branches on the riverbanks.

I can sometimes catch a trout in Ketchum with an artificial stone fly, but to see the real ones, I have to be on less populated parts of the river. If stone flies were allowed to flourish in Ketchum, people would be miserable, plagued by thick clouds of insects everywhere they went, and so a compromise has been reached. The insect population is kept down to a bearable level in town but is allowed to thrive enough outside town to sustain a trout population.

Farther out of town the mountains are enormous, the wild-life thrilling. My boots crunch through snowy banks as I make my way down to the Big Wood and carefully lower myself into its clear, rushing stream, to become part of something magnificent. The trout are there, they jump up and laugh at me, showing off their rainbow colors, but in less than a second they are gone, like a dream you recall that might have been real. Sometimes one will grab one of my ridiculous-looking fake insects and, despite its small size, put up a long and powerful fight. When I finally catch one, I admire its colors, carefully remove the hook, and gently return the fish to its river. On days when I catch a few and on days when I catch nothing, I leave the river a happy man. What could possibly be a better day?

Gray professor fly

I

Why?

Many men go fishing all their lives without knowing that it is not fish they are after.

—HENRY DAVID THOREAU

I had taken seven fish. The takers were all solid, confident, and deep. I released all the fish, and by the time I'd hiked out of the boggy forest that night, I could feel glory all around me.

—THOMAS MCGUANE, *THE LONGEST SILENCE*

Two difficult questions that I am frequently asked are why do I write and why do I fish. I would like to be able to say that the two questions are related, but I don't think that is true. All they have in common is that they are both activities that I have been impulsively drawn to for as long as I can remember. I started both when I was a boy, writing longhand with a pencil and fishing with a reasonably straight stick from a tree branch, some string, a hook, and some earthworms dug up for bait.

While some writers famously fish, many just as famously don't. Tolstoy, Steinbeck, and many other writers have judged fishing harshly. Being a good writer will not necessarily make you a good angler and there is certainly no guarantee that being skillful at fishing will make you a good writer. The only thing the two have in common is a love of solitude and a tendency for reflection. They often, but not always, attract the same type of people.

Fishing, and especially fly fishing, is about asking questions: Should you take the fish? Should you fish on a sunny or overcast day? In the river or from the riverbank? With colorful flies or not? What do these fish like to eat? At what time of day? These types of questions are endless, but underlying them all is a more fundamental question, the question of all questions: Why do it? Was nineteenth-century president Grover Cleveland right when he stated that the urge to fish was driven by "an occult and mysterious instinct"?

In my case, I think he was. Whenever I see a body of water, I look for fish. When I am by the sea, I follow bird flight patterns because birds follow fish. When I am by a river, I stare into the glassy still pools by the sides of swift-moving currents, examining the ripples enlivening the surface. I always ask where the fish are, and when I think I know, I want to try to catch them. It is an almost involuntary response—like a cat sensing the presence of a mouse.

This primordial urge started when I was such a young boy that I suspect I was born with it. It was not cultural. None of my adult relatives fished or even thought about fishing. They were all urban, not outdoors, people. My grandfather used to wear a suit, tie, and hat when we took him to the beach.

The only intersection of fishing and literature in my boyhood was that a good spot for reading and a good spot for fishing were the two things I asked of a natural setting. My primary reason for fishing was always clear: it was to go someplace beautiful where I could feel immersed in nature. I grew up in an industrial suburb of Hartford, Connecticut—not a beautiful spot. At the end of the block where I lived was a stop for city buses that went into downtown Hartford in a matter of minutes. But there was no bus that I knew of that went to nature.

The Real Estate section of the *New York Times* recently ran an article on my hometown, Newington, saying how it was one place where real estate prices hadn't gone up. But the article cautioned that the town's houses weren't especially desirable and that it had no pleasant green spaces. That's not how I remember it. I remember a park with a pond that had the predictable name of Mill Pond. The *New York Times* may not have thought this pond worth mentioning, but I remember it as a wonderful haven with a small waterfall and large rocks that were my favorite reading spot. The pond was my one contact with nature in a town surrounded by factories. And then one day I saw a flash of color in the dark water below my feet. I could hardly believe it.

My hometown had no tackle shop, but only two blocks from Mill Pond was what was called a "five and dime store," though even then there were few items that cost only five or ten cents. The store had a little of everything, and there I bought some small metal hooks, two small lead weights, a red-and-white plastic floater, and a ball of string. I knew where to find earthworms because I liked to play with them (pull them apart and you have two) and I put a worm on a hook and tied it to a piece of string tied to another string with the floater attached to it. Next I found a fallen tree branch and tied the string to it. Up until the eighteenth century, this was how people fished. They had better line than my string, but there were no reels. They just tied hooks to their lines—and tied their lines to the ends of poles.

Of course, I knew nothing of this history. I was just improvising, but it worked! The floater kept the hooked worm dangling in midwater. I felt a tug and flipped the line to shore, to land a small yellow sunfish with a splash of red on its throat. Then I caught another. And another.

Then I had an idea: there must be something living on the bottom of the pond, I thought, and it would have to feed on the midwater fish, so whatever was down there would probably like to eat my little sunfish and was probably larger than it, too. Fishing is all about understanding the fish's point of view. Who knew what monsters lay in the depths of Mill Pond?

I took off my red-and-white floater, put weights on the line, and dropped it in the lake with the sunfish still on the hook. I dragged the line across the bottom slowly . . . and there was a jerk. I instantly snapped my stick rod up and onto the shore, to see a black crayfish clinging to the sunfish by a claw.

I don't think people in Connecticut ate crayfish or even knew they lived in their waters. Crayfish certainly weren't part of the culture of the Greater Hartford Area, as it was always called.

My brother, who was not interested in pleasant reading spots but liked the idea of fishing, joined me soon after that day, which was how I first learned of the joys of fishing camaraderie. We would fill coffee cans with sunfish and crayfish and bring them home to our mother. She refused to cook any of them and made us throw away our catch.

Why had I wanted to catch those fish? I kept doing it even though in time I threw them all back because I knew I had no market. I think I fished because it was a way to more fully experience being in the wilds of Mill Pond.

Fishing for me has always been about being involved in nature. For hunters, the best hunters, it is the same thing. I went hunting only once. I had a friend in the Utah Rockies who kept inviting me to hunt with him. But I deeply dislike guns, and for aesthetic, not political, reasons. Their noise makes my ears ring, and I do not appreciate the punch in the shoulder that comes with a recoiling rifle. I also don't like the idea of shooting an animal from a long distance. There is no involvement with nature or the creature in that, and so it is a fraud.

Then my friend and I came up with the idea of bow hunting. It takes some skill to stalk an animal until you are close enough to shoot it with a bow and arrow. I flew to Utah and stalked for a week, learning everything I could about the high mountains surrounding me, about which trails a doe would take and which a buck, and how a buck will distract you so that you won't stalk his family. The buck's misconception seemed unfair. How could he understand that we were only permitted to shoot bucks, not their families. It was like learning about fishing, about rivers and about fish. But then I shot a buck who looked up at me with big soft deer eyes as his legs buckled and he collapsed. Not being of the stuff that true hunters are made of, I petted him on the head and told him I was sorry. I never did that with a fish, although I do sometimes admonish a fish to be more careful before I put it back in the river. I never again wanted to shoot a mammal.

I think that the closer we are to an animal biologically, the more sentimental we are about it. Why do we care more about marine mammals than fish? I once hooked a seal by the flipper with a bass plug I had cast in San Francisco Bay and felt terrible for days, but had I hooked a bass as I intended, I would have felt wonderful.

Perhaps the difference is in the eyes. Mammal eyes seem designed to fill us with guilt, whereas fish eyes seem to be about nothing more than being alert. Only a salmon's eyes can sometimes seem to look angry or panic-stricken.

The American poet Elizabeth Bishop once wrote about a caught fish for whom she felt sympathy:

> I looked into his eyes
> Which were far larger than mine
> But shallower, and yellowed,
> The irises backed and packed
> With tarnished tinfoil
> Seen through the lenses
> Of old scratched isinglass.

Eyes of tarnished foil. Not plaintive eyes, like a deer's. Not even pleading eyes, like a sea otter's.

President Jimmy Carter, a lifelong hunter and fisherman, admitted that on occasion even he felt stricken with guilt. Then he added, "For people who might find these feelings overwhelming, my advice would be: 'Don't hunt or fish.'"

If you fish in order to participate in nature, then what is your role? You are a predator and since your prey is also a predator, you are a predator's predator. You must think like your prey in order to succeed. The bait, the plug, and the fly are all designed to appeal to the predatory instinct of a fish. You are the predator tricking this killer. Joan Wulff, a legendary fly fisher and the wife of another legendary and famously competitive fly fisher, Lee Wulff, wrote of the predator instinct: "The best anglers I know are those who can most easily relate to this whole natural process."

Stalking a trout is similar to stalking a deer, and though I have little experience with bird-watching, I suppose its appeal is that it is a way of stalking nature without being a predator. But since a bird-watcher is not a predator, he or she is not fully participating in nature, which is fundamentally about predator and prey.

So, while fishers have written volumes about the angler's virtues and high character, much of which may be true, there is also a certain ruthlessness involved. Novelist and dedicated fly fisherman Thomas McGuane wrote, "The fisherman now is one who defies society, who rips lips, who drains the pool, who takes no prisoners."

One day I was fishing the smooth, wide Snake River in Wyoming. Around me rose the muscular, glaciered rock giants of the Grand Tetons, standing strong above the clouds. Each had its own personality—the Grand Teton majestic, the Nez Perce sharp and dangerous, the Mount Owen sprawling, scarred, almost avuncular. And that was enough for me. Trout were just an excuse.

I was studying the currents, catching cutthroat trout. I caught one every third or fourth cast, took it off the hook, gently eased it back into the current, and cast again. I might have been doing this for an hour or for three. I always wear a waterproof watch while fishing, but I always forget to look at it. Time does not exist when you are on the river. But fatigue does, and I needed a break. I waded to the bank and sat down next to my companion, who was also taking a break.

Snake River, Wyoming, by the Grand Tetons, good spot for cutthroat trout

As I sat down, he smiled at me and said, "Winning feels good, doesn't it?"

Though I would never have put it that way, I had to admit that this was what I was feeling. If you do it right, outsmarting a trout or a salmon with a little clump of feathers on a hook is no small accomplishment. The fish wins most of the time. On this day only about 65 percent of the time, but on other days, often 90 percent or even 100 percent. So, fishing is a little bit about winning and losing.

There are many fishing competitions that have nothing to do with being in nature or even catching fish, but everything about winning and losing. There are fly-casting competitions and fly-tying competitions, and sometimes the contestants are not even anglers, just people who enjoy participating in competitive sports.

Competitive fly-casting, usually for distance, was invented in the United States in the 1860s, with some of the first matches held in New York and Chicago. Casting clubs that organized national competitions had developed by the 1880s, and in 1907 these clubs united under the National Association of Scientific Casting Clubs. The association then arranged competitions, not in good fishing spots, but at prestigious sites like the reflecting pool in front of the Lincoln Memorial in Washington, D.C. These competitions had little to do with fishing, but if you could claim to be a national casting champion, it improved your standing as a fisher.

FOR MANY CENTURIES, fly fishing enthusiasts have ascribed extravagant virtues to their fellow casters. Gervase Markham, a sixteenth-to-seventeenth-century English mercenary soldier who wrote poetry and wrote on food and cooking and horse breeding, was an enthusiastic fly fisherman. This is what he wrote about fly fishers:

> Any angler must be a scholar and a grammarian, able to write and discourse on his art in true and fitting terms; he must have sweetness of speech to entice others to delight in so laudable an exercise, and strength of argument to defend it against envy and slander; he must be strong and valiant, neither to be amazed with storms nor affrighted to thunder; and his is not temperate but has a gnawing stomach, he will not endure fasting but must observe hours.

To that description, I would add: he must have good hand–eye coordination.

Others have seen different traits in fly fishers. Sir Humphry Davy, the brilliant father of modern chemistry, weighed in on this. For more than a century Davy, who was born in 1778, was the hero of British boy science nerds. A great nerd and the original "Mr. Wizard," he separated, discovered, and named critical elements that were often too unstable to separate including sodium, potassium, iodine, calcium, magnesium, strontium, and barium. He developed a new grade of high explosives with nitrogen and chlorine. He also developed electric batteries and many other new miracles. He delighted the public with lectures in which he demonstrated his many discoveries, especially how to get high on nitrous oxide, later to be called "laughing gas." Famous personalities attended his lectures, including the poet Samuel Taylor Coleridge and Mary Shelley, who was inspired by his talks to develop her mad scientist Dr. Frankenstein. But once he became Britain's leading scientist he became embroiled in a bitter struggle over his belief that scientists should be serious professionals and not aristocratic dilettantes.

Davy's great retreat from this intense intellectual and political life was to free himself from thinking by fly fishing for salmon. He even wrote a book on it, *Salmonia: or Days of Fly Fishing*. The book is packed with observations from his years of fishing. The science is not always as accurate as would be expected but much less was known about salmon then. He insisted on the high caliber of people who choose to fly fish:

> Most art may be said to characterize man in his highest or intellectual state; and the fisher for salmon and trout with the fly employs not only machinery to assist his

physical powers, but applies sagacity to conquer difficulties; and the pleasures derived from ingenious resources and devices, as well as from active pursuit, belongs to this amusement.

In other words, according to one of the great scientific minds of the nineteenth century, to be a good fly fisher, you need to be very smart. And that is not all. Davy believed that fly fishing also required a strong scientific background, an understanding of fish and the animals they eat, knowledge of weather patterns and the life of the river, and character. "It is a pursuit of moral discipline," he wrote, "requiring patience, forbearance and command of temper."

Writer and environmental activist Robert H. Boyle, founder of a number of organizations to preserve the Hudson River, once said, "I owe whatever I have done for this world to the fact that I am a fisherman who, out of necessity, became deeply involved in the workings and protection of nature."

Some even assert that if you want your children to grow up to be environmentalists, you must take them fishing. This is a dubious claim. While some hunters and fishers are serious conservationists, it cannot be argued that they lead the environmental movement. President Grover Cleveland was one of the more active fishermen to occupy the White House (he endeared himself to the South by ignoring a Civil War commemoration and going fishing instead), but he could not be considered an environmentalist.

President Herbert Hoover, a dedicated fly fisher, took time off from his 1928 presidential campaign to fish for steelhead in the Rogue and Klamath rivers. Long out of office in 1963, he published a book titled *Fishing for Fun and to Wash Your Soul,* in which he wrote: "A fisherman must be of contemplative mind for it is often a long time between bites. Those interregnums emanate patience, reserve, and calm-reflection."

Fisherfolk can't help praising other fishers. Joan Wulff, famously married to Lee Wulff, claimed, "This is also a sport that strengthens relationships. If you can fish with someone you can probably live with them happily. Fishing is a test of your values. Most fly fishermen are thoughtful, sensitive, caring individuals."

Most, perhaps, but certainly not all. Francisco Franco, who ruled over Spain for thirty-six years with relentless brutality, was an avid fly fisherman. In fact, one of the few positive things he ever did for Spain was protecting the salmon runs in the northern Spanish rivers.

Many believe in the healing powers of fly fishing. An organization called Project Healing Waters Fly Fishing tries to help veterans with emotional, psychological, and physical problems by taking them fly fishing regularly. Similarly, Casting for Recovery aims to help women with breast cancer by organizing retreats built around breast cancer education and fly fishing.

So many presidents have been fly fishermen that a correlation between the sport and politics has been suggested. But it has also been suggested that it is good politics to be seen fly fishing—that being an angler makes a politician seem more appealing. Hoover declared that a number of presidents—including McKinley, Taft, Wilson, Harding, Coolidge, Franklin Roosevelt, and Truman—had not been serious fishermen before being elected, but once in office liked being seen and photographed fishing. Novelist John Steinbeck once observed, in what is certainly an exaggeration, "No candidate would think of running for office without first catching and

John Quincy Adams's fly wallet, nineteenth century

being photographed with a fish. A nonfisherman could not be elected President."

Though Calvin Coolidge was a native Vermonter, he was apparently not a very good fly fisherman. According to Hoover, "Then Mr. Coolidge took to a fly. He gave the Secret Service guards great excitement in dodging his back cast and rescuing flies from trees." There were many photographs of the unfortunate casts, and soon thereafter Coolidge declared that he would not run for president again, opening the path to the White House for Hoover.

When fishing on a river with overgrown banks, it is not unusual for back casts to end up in trees. However, a number of casts have been designed to cope with such situations, and if Coolidge didn't know a roll cast or Spey cast, Hoover may have been right: Coolidge may not have been a very experienced fisherman. But Hoover's belittling of his predecessor's back cast may have had more to do with Coolidge's refusal to endorse him than with fishing; Coolidge even said of Hoover at one point, "For six years that man has given me unsolicited advice—all of it bad."

Hoover listed himself, Grover Cleveland, and Theodore Roosevelt as the only "life-long fly fishermen" to have served as U.S. president. (George Washington, Chester Arthur, and Dwight Eisenhower also fished, but not with flies.) Cleveland refused to buy his country home in Buzzards Bay, Massachusetts, until the celebrated actor Joseph Jefferson assured him that the fishing was good there.

Hoover also claimed that fishing is healthy for U.S. presidents. He wrote, "Fishing reduces the ego in Presidents and former Presidents, for at fishing most men are not equal to boys." This is probably true since even the most powerful man in the world cannot command a trout or salmon to take his fly.

Furthermore, Hoover believed that fishing kept people with criminal tendencies off the streets. He wrote, "Lots of people committed crimes during the year who would not have done so if they had been fishing."

Jimmy Carter, though not a "life-long fisherman," belongs on the list of presidents who were authentic fly fishermen. He grew up hunting and fishing in rural southern Georgia. But the kinds of fish to catch with flies, chiefly trout and salmon, don't live in warm water, and so it wasn't until Carter was elected governor of Georgia and moved to Atlanta that he starting fishing with flies; he once described himself as having arrived in Atlanta "piscatorially retarded." The governor's mansion was only a few miles from the cold-water Chattahoochee River and there Carter took his first fly rod, accompanied by the head of the Georgia Fish and Game Commission.

Once Carter discovered fly fishing, he never stopped, and he later described it as one of the best-kept secret activities of his presidency. He wrote:

> We often landed in the helicopter at Camp David, changed clothes while the White House press corps departed to a nearby Maryland town, and then secretly took off again to land forty minutes later in a pasture alongside Spruce Creek in Pennsylvania for a couple of days of secluded fly fishing.

Carter was the third president to write a book about fishing and his, *An Outdoor Journal*, is the best of the three. He wrote:

> To be able to present the proper fly to a rising fish demands the greatest degree of determination, study, planning, and practice, and there is always something more to discover. In the woods or on a stream, my concentration is so intense that for long periods the rest of the world is almost forgotten.

While this obsessive perfectionism and intensity is typical Carter, as anyone who made the mistake of trying to play softball with him will tell you, there is a basic truth here. Fly fishing is for the curious. Every river is different; every beat on each river is different; every river has its own fish, shape, and bottom; and every river sings its own song. I think I was born loving the sea, but fly fishing has taught me to love rivers.

Every time you fish, you learn something new. There is no end to it. The fisher who thinks he or she knows everything knows nothing. As the Irish poet William Butler Yeats said about love:

> There is nobody wise enough
> To find out all that is in it,
> For he would be thinking of love
> Till the stars had run away
> and the shadows eaten the moon.

I stand in the middle of a stunningly beautiful river, letting the birdsong trill counterpoint to what Western writer and fishing enthusiast Zane Grey once called the river's "melodious roar," which is sometimes not a roar, but a whisper or a gurgle or a coo. I feel the river's water pushing insistently against my legs. I am thinking about my casts, about how they land, where they land, how they drift, and where the fish are and what they want. I am immersed in what Tolstoy, describing the joys of mowing hay, called "moments of oblivion." This is all I am thinking about and this is as close as I come to not thinking at all and that gives me a special kind of peace.

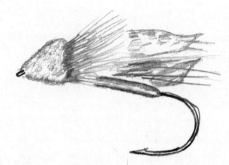

Muddler minnow fly

2

Doing It the Hard Way

It has always been my conviction that anyone who pits his intelligence against a fish and loses, has it coming.

—JOHN STEINBECK, "ON FISHING"

F ly fishing is a contrarian conceit. All other types of fishing try to facilitate the catching of fish; fly fishing is about making it as difficult as possible. But once you have caught a fish with an artificial fly, all other types of fishing may seem like cheating. President Dwight Eisenhower put it simply, saying, "I don't use worms. I want fishing to be a challenge."

Steinbeck, who underestimated the intelligence of salmonids (trout, salmon, and char), failed to appreciate that while anyone can catch a fish with a net and probably with bait, it is extremely difficult to catch one with an artificial fly. Or maybe he did appreciate that but felt that if you failed to catch anything while fly fishing, it served you right for choosing such a difficult fishing method. Maybe, too, he was right and we do have it coming, which is why we so easily forgive ourselves when we fail to catch anything.

Fly fishing is done only for sport. It would be a dumb way to catch fish for any practical purpose, and it is for this reason that many Native Americans are contemptuous of fly fishing. Yes, a few have become proficient at it in places like Alaska, where being a fly fishing guide is the best job available, but most think that the purpose of fishing is to catch fish for food. It is a gift from the gods, and to play with it for recreation is disrespectful.

Native Americans use a tremendous variety of fishing techniques, but you will rarely see them fly fishing. They net, sometimes with a dip net—a small net on a long pole—and they spear, as Europeans did centuries ago. Today, spear fishing is generally thought to be too efficient and is usually illegal, yet many who have tried it have said that it was a thrill. Fly fishing guru Lee Wulff said that when he was growing up in Alaska, "Spearing was the most fun. It was challenging to judge a fish's speed and take into account the index of refraction when striking while the salmon were swimming past at fifteen or twenty miles an hour."

Native Americans also sometimes fish using no tackle at all. Near Nondalton, Alaska, in a river that runs into Bristol Bay, I saw young boys wade out, their fingers spread like fighting bear claws over the water, and at just the right second, rush in, grab a salmon or trout, and toss it onto the bank, where it writhed like an angry patient in a straitjacket.

If you are Hoover's kind of fisherman, a "life-long fisherman," you will probably end up going in one of two directions. Either you will end up infatuated with size and the fight involved in catching a fish, and so will pursue marlin and other giant fish, or you will become a dedicated fly fisher. For completely different reasons, these are the two hardest ways to fish—the first because it is the hardest way to land a fish and the second because it is the hardest way to hook a fish.

This split is personified by two Hemingway men. Ernest, the author, was raised in the outdoors life by his father, who introduced him to all kinds of hunting and fishing, including fly fishing. But although Ernest wrote about fly fishing several times, he was never a devotee. He was happy to simply use bait, and when he fly fished, he used wet flies, not the aficionado's choice. He also fly fished with two "drops," meaning three flies at a time; a drop is an additional fly. And once he discovered marlin fishing in the Gulf Stream, fly fishing was pretty much over for him, though he occasionally fly fished in Idaho between hunting trips.

Ernest's oldest son, Jack, on the other hand, was not interested in chasing big marlin—or in hunting, his father's other great passion. All Jack really wanted was to fly fish. He settled in Ketchum, where he earned the reputation of being one of the world's truly great fly fishers.

Anyone who doubts Jack's fly fishing obsession should examine his World War Two record, when he served as a spy for the OSS. He parachuted into the south of France behind German lines carrying with him a fly rod. Parachuting with a fly rod is no easy feat: How to land without breaking it? Jack's solution was to tie it to twenty feet of line and let go of it just before landing.

He was dropped from fourteen hundred feet, a very high jump, and landed in a rocky ravine, with both his rod and his body intact. He made contact with the French underground, and whenever he could, he fished. When on the run, he made notes of promising streams with good gravel beds, pools, and banks to which he might be able to return one day.

Later, Jack was wounded and taken prisoner. The Germans told him that his arm had to be amputated or he could die from gangrene. He refused the offer, explaining that his wounded arm was his casting arm and he would rather die than lose it. Both Jack and his arm survived to fish many more streams, and many who later fished with him said, "Jack didn't ever want to quit. There was always one more cast to try."

In contrast to fly fishing, big-game fishing is all about catching the largest fish. Maybe it's about the photo. There you are, dwarfed beside a thousand-pound marlin hanging next to you. That's a lot more impressive than holding up a thirty-five-pound salmon. Of course, paradoxically, the fisher looks a lot bigger beside the thirty-five-pound salmon than he or she does beside a thousand-pound marlin.

Henry David Thoreau once explained that he recorded the weight of the pickerel he caught on Walden Pond because "the weight of a fish is commonly his only title to fame." Official world-record weights are documented for almost all game fish. The world-record black marlin was caught in 1953 off Cabo Blanco, Peru, and weighed 1,560 pounds. The world-record brook trout was caught in 1915 on the Nipigon River in the Thunder Bay area of Ontario and weighed fourteen and a half pounds. The black marlin was caught with live bait after a fight of an hour and forty-five minutes, whereas the brook trout was caught with a fly and landed in just a few minutes. Brook trout are not one of the hardest-fighting fish.

Once I learned of the alternatives, I was never much drawn to bait fishing. John Steinbeck, though he may not have realized it, was on to something. If the fish are easily outsmarted, fishing is joyless. To dangle food in front of a fish so that he will smell it and try to eat it is not a great challenge, though even this is not as easy as it sounds, because the ocean is vast and you have to find the fish before you can catch it.

Though I have never owned a boat, I have gone out with friends who had boats and fished with live bait. In San Francisco, where I lived for a time, a friend and I would take a boat out in the bay and troll around the bridge pilings in search of fish. It was hard to fail at this because striped bass fed on the mollusks on the pilings and you were sure to entice a few to take your bait. In Gloucester, Massachusetts, where I was a part-time resident for a while, we would also do well when fishing off a boat at the mouth of Gloucester Harbor where the stripers came in to feed.

The only time I can recall fishing with bait from a boat and catching nothing was in the Pacific fishing port of Guaymas, Mexico. I was moving to Mexico City and stopped off in Guaymas because I can never resist a fishing port. I settled on a price with a lean, hard-working young man to take me out in his brightly painted, well-dented aluminum outboard. Like most fishermen, this man lived on hope. He hoped his little beat-up boat would attract a tourist if he painted it in bright colors, and then he hoped he would catch some fish.

We headed out to sea with cut-up fish in the mackerel family for bait. But I caught nothing. The sun was setting rosy and yellow, the way it does over the Pacific after a hot day. It was time to go in.

The young man refused.

I fished some more, but still caught nothing and now it was a moonless, starlit dark night. Then it occurred to me that the young man was probably hoping to catch fish to take home to his family. I told him that I would pay him extra so that he could buy food if he would take us in.

No, he wanted a fish.

Like most people living on hope, he was very insistent.

I fished on, but still caught nothing, until finally in the black of night with no light on the boat and a certain sense of humiliation or defeat, the young man headed us back to shore.

Some days, as the saying goes, "they aren't biting." That does not happen often when fishing with bait from a boat, but with other types of rod fishing, the odds are stacked against you to a far greater degree.

For years, my preferred method of fishing was surf-casting, which is the premier blue-collar fishing technique used in New England by fishers who do not own boats. We used twelve- or fourteen-foot rods to cast painted wooden, metal, or fiberglass plugs that would either sink to midwater or swim the surface, depending on how you played them. Everyone had their own favorite plugs; there aren't as many plugs as there are flies to choose from, but there's still a wide variety. Some are lighter, some are heavier, some metallic, some white, some green. Some resemble a minnow or herring. Some do not look like any known fish.

Surf-casting, as the name implies, is all about casting. The challenge is to cast the plug as far out into the ocean as possible. If you are good, you can cast out as far as fishers on a boat might go. The plug usually has a blunt or concave head and is sometimes in two parts. This gives it movement as you reel it in, and the farther you have cast, the more water you have to play the plug. You can also invent small movements with the rod to increase the activity of the plug, in the hopes of attracting the fish.

Stripers and blues define New England surf-casting. Stripers, striped bass, are harder to catch, as they're more selective. Bluefish are either feeding or they aren't. If they are, mayhem often erupts, with the bait fish driven to the surface by the hunting blues, birds swooping down to fight the bluefish for the bait, and the sharp-toothed bluefish slashing at whatever comes by their mouths. You could catch a dozen of them if you could cast fast and far enough.

I have always loved casting and I could enjoy hours on a beautiful coastline not catching a single fish, but perfecting my cast. I did this in Connecticut, Rhode Island, Nantucket, and Martha's Vineyard, Gloucester, and further north. Wherever I was near a beautiful coastline, I fished. When I lived in San Francisco, it was a short walk from my apartment on the marina to the beach alongside the old Presidio. I had picked the neighborhood for its proximity to the fishing spot. With the Golden Gate off to my left and the Bay to my right, I cast in the blushing early morning light.

One summer I had a job as the pastry maker for a restaurant in Nantucket. I had my own kitchen and would arrive at dawn, greeted only by the owner's cat, to whom I gave a small bowl of cream. By noon I had produced a wagon filled with Austro-Hungarian cakes, French pastries, and assorted Italian pastries. At about the time the customers started arriving, I had left and was on my bike, balancing my fly rod in one hand as I headed out of town. In those days Nantucket wasn't as overbuilt as it is today, and once you left town you were on wild uninhabited moors where the fog struggled to pass over spikey brush. I would go to a beach called Surfside, wade into the sea, and surf-cast for the rest of the day. That was a good summer.

I probably caught around fifty fish in my surf-casting years, but this was after more than one thousand casts.

I did not understand then how close surf-casting is to fly fishing. I sometimes even used a fly when I surf-cast. I would tie the fly to the back hook of my bass plug and the movement of the plug would play the fly. The striper usually took the fly, not the plug. But I never considered fly fishing.

For one thing, you don't fly fish in the ocean. I was never interested in fishing in rivers and lakes. But a greater deterrent was that I thought of fly fishing as something that wealthy people, and especially wealthy snobs, did. This is partly because American fly fishing is derived from British fly fishing and in Great Britain, this is clearly true. In England the rights to a river are held by the owners of the river's banks, who are usually landed gentry. In Scotland, rivers are separate property, not necessarily connected to their banks, and a river owner can sell or rent their river. It is very difficult to find a beat on which you can fish unless you know an aristocrat, though a few owners take pride in making their river available to others. The Helmsdale, in the Scottish Highlands, where Prince Charles likes to fish, is a river whose owners are proud of letting the locals fish on occasion, but this is to have fish to supply eggs and milt for their hatchery. But only a few river owners genuinely welcome locals or outside anglers and then only after they have paid large fees.

At one time in England, there was a tradition of working-class fly fishers, but once the last of the Enclosure Acts, as the laws that made fishing rivers private property are known, were passed in the early twentieth century, millions of acres had been fenced off from ordinary people.

Steinbeck opined that while the French fished for relaxation and the Americans saw it as a contest between man and nature, the British fly fished as a way of expressing "the English Passion for private property." Such generalizations may contain some truth, but are always problematic. When Steinbeck described the French fishers, he was talking about the Parisians he knew who left the city from time to time for some quiet time on a river. But I can assure you that the Frenchmen with whom I went barracuda fishing in the deep pockets, or *bolongs*, of the Saloum River in Senegal were die-hard fishermen not at all interested in relaxation.

Similarly, some British fishermen are very much into the battle between man and nature, and some Americans suffer from as much elitism as the British. William Trotter Porter, a leading American sports journalist in the mid-nineteenth century, wrote, "Fly fishing has been designated the royal and aristocratic branch of the angler's craft and unquestionably it is the most difficult, the most elegant, and to men of taste, by myriad of degrees the most exciting and pleasant mode of angling."

What did Porter mean by "men of taste"? Probably not me or the people with whom I went surf-casting, and clearly not women.

In Britain and to a limited degree in the United States, fly fishing is organized around fly fishing clubs, some of which have huge snob appeal. London's Flyfishers' Club, founded in 1884, counts royals among its members and offers private dining.

Fly fishing clubs on both continents have not allowed women to join until recently. President Cleveland had the habit of referring to fly fishers as a "fraternity," and as he was opposed to equal rights for African Americans, he probably would not have welcomed people of color into his fraternity either.

Though fly fishing equipment is usually not expensive, the sport is often a rich man's game. Only the wealthy are heli-coptered in to fly fish in Russia's pristine Kola Peninsula; they pay many thousands of dollars for the trip. Many places from Alaska to New Brunswick provide luxury lodges aimed at wealthy fly fishers.

To fish in order to test yourself against a fish rather than catch it does at first glance seem to be a rich man's game. But on a deeper level, fly fishing is about submerging yourself in the natural order, in the world of predator and prey, and there could be nothing less elitist than that. In the United States, no one owns the rivers and anyone who pays a small fee to a state's fish and game commission has the right to fish.

Whatever a sport's origin, it usually does not remain an elitist activity in America unless it involves very costly equip-ment such as a horse or yacht. The German philosopher Hannah Arendt once wrote that one of the most surprising things about America for Europeans was that Americans really do believe in "the pursuit of happiness" as an inalienable right. It's a profound part of how Americans think, and it would be absolutely un-American for fly fishing to be limited to the wealthy. In recent decades, in fact, as fly fishing has become increasingly popular, it has been becoming increasingly popu-list as well.

Fly fishing first caught my attention because I used to read Red Smith's sports column in the *New York Times*. Smith crafted his columns with the flair and panache of a great short story writer and although I first started reading him because of my interest in baseball, I started noticing that he frequently wrote about fly fishing as well. Smith had a great fondness for the Beaverkill River in upstate New York. He called it "the cradle of fly fishing in America," because of the many nineteenth- and twentieth-century greats who had fished there. He would often take note of the day that fly fishing season opened, and he once wrote, "It can be said without irreverence that to celebrate Opening Day on the Beaverkill is a little like observing Christmas in Bethlehem."

Fly fishing's opening day has been celebrated all over the world for centuries, though it wasn't always referred to exactly as such. Ancient cultures in Europe and Asia celebrated the first fish of the season, and Native Americans who fish salmon—Atlantic or Pacific—all have a salmon ceremony at the start of each fishing year. When Maine's Penobscot River was still rich in salmon, anglers would send the first catch of the river's Bangor Pool to the president of the United States, starting with William Howard Taft. Actually, Taft got the second fish that year because two were caught in quick succession and as the first was quite large, it was sold to the Clark Thread company in Newark, New Jersey, which paid a high price per pound. Taft's fish was an eleven pounder, five pounds smaller than the first fish.

In Ireland children play hooky from school on the opening day of the brown trout season. And in Galway, on the wide shallow River Corrib that rushes through the town to Galway Bay, the first salmon of the season is donated to charity. The second can be kept by the angler. So, with customary Irish humor, fishers in Galway say as opening day approaches, "I hope you catch the second fish."

Opening day on the Beaverkill, as described by Red Smith, seemed like a good enough reason to me to take up fly fishing.

But I didn't start fishing on an opening day or on the Beaverkill. My first experience was on the Ausable River in New York's Adirondacks. Eastern rivers are difficult to fish because their banks are overgrown, and at first I was forever hooking my flies in tree branches. Wider rivers with more open banks out west worked better. But in time I learned that it is on eastern rivers that you really learn how to cast.

After fly fishing for years, I finally celebrated an opening day, but not in New York—in Norway, where opening day begins at the stroke of midnight. I went out with a group of Norwegians who were in a festive mood. They had a late-night picnic that included a great deal of beer on a bank of the Stjørdal River, which has both rough rapids and calm glassy pools. Loud melodious birds sang as the river grew darker. At the stroke of midnight, there was a Nordic cheer and everyone began casting. I cast only two or three times. Fishing in the dark makes little sense unless you know the river well. Then I and most of the other fishers returned to camp to go to sleep. We had observed opening day and tomorrow we would fish. But a few anglers stayed through the night, drinking and fishing and sleeping in chairs. At four in the morning one of them landed a brown trout. No one landed a salmon.

I always think of fly fishing as a recent hobby of mine, something I took up later in life, after I had left the ocean and years of surf-casting. Actually, though, I took it up in my mid-twenties, in New York State, Basque Country, and Scotland, which means I have been a fly fisherman for forty years.

I have fly fished all over the world. That is the ultimate refinement of the Steinbeck dictum. Fishing a new river makes catching a fish as difficult as possible. If you lose, as Steinbeck said, you have it coming, but if you win you have earned it.

Ray Bergman, whose book *Trout* is many fishers' bible, wrote, "It is a good rule to always blame yourself if you have poor luck. Be unmerciful in your judgment of *you*—of the way you fish, in the way you fish, in the place you fish, in every motion you make."

Nonetheless, excuses have become a standard part of fly fishing humor. The water was too high, too low, too fast, too slow, too muddy; the sky was too cloudy, too sunny. I have used all these excuses. So has everyone else. And they can be true problems. But the point is that if you fail, you fail because you didn't compensate for these challenges. I have also caught fish in all of these situations.

For a fisherman to be playing fair, the fish must be given a fighting chance because that is the definition of the natural order. Part of the intrigue is that each time you make your way to the river, you don't know if it will be a day of plenty or a day of nothing. Eagles, bears, and other predators face the day with similar doubts. Only humans think they can shorten the odds. So why not submit to a natural challenge: fairly match your intelligence against that of a fish and see who wins.

There is an element of luck but it is foolish to wait for it or blame it for failure. As Santiago, the old fisherman in Hemingway's *The Old Man and the Sea*, said, "It is better to be lucky. But I would rather be exact. Then when luck comes, you are ready."

When you wade into a river, you have truly entered a world of dazzling beauty. Now, though, you have to understand the river.

First, you listen to it. A river is a choral ensemble with gurgling treble voices and rumbling bass waves underneath. It is as loud as strong human voices. Some fishermen think the river speaks

to them. I think it sings. Poet
William Carlos Williams wrote
that a poem was "an ensemble
of tides, waves, and ripples." So
then, in reverse, isn't a river a
poem?

Human visitors are not
always welcome on a river.
Salmon are a favorite food of
large and dangerous brown
bears, called by the more

*A trout takes a fly and tries to
pull it out*

descriptive name of "grizzly bears" in Alaska. These very large
creatures can kill you with one swipe of a paw. So I have some
reservations about having them as fishing company. Alaskans
seem to feel differently. Guides often offer the presence of bears
along a river as a great attraction. "I will take you to a river full
of bears," they sometimes say. One guide even suggested to me
that we fish in a place where the bears chase your fish as you
reel it in—like a cat with a toy. But getting into a dispute with
a bear over a fish did not strike me as a good idea.

Most of the time bears just watch fly fishermen, wondering
what they could possibly be doing. The elk that stare down
from the mountain slopes of the Big Wood seem to have similar
thoughts. In Russia on the Ozernaya in the Pacific peninsula
of Kamchatka, I had the impression that the bears were thinking
what the cuckoo birds were saying. Cuckoo birds, it turns out,
sound exactly like those German clocks. Even if I was just
comic relief I was still part of this natural world. Surely a bear
who sticks a snout or paw in the river and snags a passing fish
has to wonder what I am doing. If she (I saw mostly sows) even
understood that I was trying to catch fish, she would have

thought that this was the most ridiculous way to catch a fish she had ever seen.

Bears are hunted in both Alaska and Russia and they probably have trouble distinguishing a fisherman from a hunter and may wonder if the waving pole is a fishing rod or a hunting rifle. I have never had a solid grasp of hunting and cannot understand why anyone would want to shoot such an inedible animal for the fun of it. But then again Tibetan Buddhist and Native Americans cannot understand why I would want to catch a fish for the fun of it.

The Russians take bears more seriously than the Alaskans. They train dogs called Laikas to protect the fishers. These handsome, shepherd-size sled dogs, white with corkscrew tails, are really not big enough to take on a brown bear, but they let out such a racket of barking and snarling when a bear approaches that the annoyed bears want nothing to do with them.

Laikas are very affectionate dogs, and once the three I met during my Russia trip realized that I was one of those people who can spend endless time petting and rubbing a dog, I had three close friends. But this did not give me any special protection. One day while rubbing one dog's belly with my right hand and the head of another dog resting in my lap with my left, I saw a very large sow waddling her way into the camp. The happy dogs, their eyes closed, didn't move.

"Come on, guys, it's bears," I shouted.

The dogs did nothing and seemed to be saying things like, "Scratch a little more to the left, please."

"Come on," I shouted again as the bear got closer. "You're supposed to chase her!" I poked them and this time they looked around, jumped up, and with a tremendous amount of growling and dog unpleasantness, started to drive the sow off. One of them even bit her in the posterior. The bear turned around with a look of indignation and rubbed her butt as she lumbered off.

What fine dogs! They guarded us all night so we could sleep. They deserved a good belly rub during the day. They had short lives, though, because when a dog starts to get old, a bear can sense its weakness and will kill it if given the chance. There is a lot of beauty but no kindness in the wilderness.

CASTING A FLY is a far more challenging proposition than casting other kinds of lures. A surf-casting lure is quite heavy and if you send it soaring, its weight will carry it and pull the line behind. But a fly is very light. It is the line, not the lure, that you have to shoot out, and if you do that well, the line will straighten out with the fly on the end of it. On a good cast, the fly will land first with the straight line behind it. Some argue that the fly does not have to land first as long as the line is straight. It depends on the fish, the type of fly, and the situation. But if a line slaps the water or is not straight, the fish will know that something is up and will avoid that thing that has just landed.

The fly must land lightly. In the short story "The Red Girl," Irish writer Maurice Walsh perfectly describes a perfect cast: "The fly at full stretch came down on the water like a caress."

Norman Maclean in his novel *A River Runs Through It* quotes one of his father's casting lessons: "It is an art that is performed on a four-count rhythm between ten and two o'clock." That is a description of an overhand cast with a one-handed rod, which works well if there are no trees or bushes behind you and the wind is not blowing in your face. But if that is not the case, you can use a roll cast, which does not go into the branches behind you, or, if you are using a two-handed European rod, sometimes called a Spey rod, a double Spey cast. The Spey cast, named after Scotland's River Spey where I fished many years ago and failed to catch anything, can also be performed with a single-handed rod. I like the double Spey cast, but it only works when the wind is blowing downriver. When the wind is blowing upriver, a roll, single Spey, or C-snap works better. There is a wide repertoire of casts for difficult situations.

Curiously, almost all casts have four beats. An overhead cast with a two-handed Spey rod has a four-count beat between twelve and two o'clock. Maclean said he learned casting with a metronome, and I sometimes listen to music in my head to get the timing right while casting. A Bach cello suite, which I have been playing on my cello for years and never gotten quite right, just like my casts, works well. Bach is reliably rhythmic. Still, his cello suite is in 3/4 time and since most casts have four beats, I also recommend rock and roll, which is usually in 4/4 time. The Rolling Stones' "I Can't Get No Satisfaction" can lead to a perfect cast.

When I first took my daughter, Talia, fly fishing, she was young and small, but I still could not help suspecting that she was casting better than I was. She had already been studying ballet for a number of years, as she has continued to do, and it had given her grace and a great sense of rhythm. Joan Wulff also came from a dance background and has said, "I am convinced that the dancing lessons improved my casting because they taught me to use my whole body to back up my limited ten-year-old strength."

Wulff also revealed an important secret when she wrote about feeling beautiful while casting. Though "the fraternity" has always insisted that fly fishing is intrinsically masculine, there is something feminine about casting flies. "The art of casting always makes me think of dancing and therefore it seems more feminine than masculine," Joan wrote. "Casting has both visual beauty and a feeling of oneness in the combination of body motion, rod action, and the weight of the flexible line. Like dancing, it can make you feel beautiful."

I wish I could go fly fishing with Nureyev. That might be an unforgettable experience.

Casting is a force that moves up on ever thinner rails. It starts with legs and hips anchored in the river, moves up the back to an arm or arms, and then enters the rod, which is tapered so that it is flexible. The force snaps the rod up and shoots the line, which is also tapered, to the leader, a thinner, also tapered extension of the line, designed to be invisible to fish. When the end of the tapered leader is fully extended, it lands in the water with the fly on its end. Joan Wulff calls a cast "a flow of energy."

Once you have executed the perfect cast, you have to execute the perfect drift. I have caught trout so hungry and over-eager that they swallowed the fly just as it was landing in the water. But usually they like to sit in the river and assess a situation before making a move. Salmon and trout will often leap in the air, sometimes all around you, but that does not mean that they will take your fly. I often feel that leaping fish are laughing at me.

You have to land your cast in the right spot. Often that is not where the fish is, but where a current will drift your cast downriver in a natural manner so that it passes right by the fish.

Fish like pools—deep still areas, often with a glassy surface, where there is not much current and they can relax. For salmon, which swim upstream against the current, a pool is a welcome break, a place where they can look for interesting objects floating past. Sometimes, too, there is a trough in the river, a long deep stretch between the bank and the middle of the river where fish can rest, look for food, or swim along as an unobstructed highway.

You have to find the right spot with the right drift and land in it perfectly. Otherwise, as Steinbeck said, you have it coming.

Spey fly

3

The Thinking Prey

After his two thousand miles, he rests,
Breathing in that lap of easy current
In his graveyard pool.

—TED HUGHES, "OCTOBER SALMON"

Fly fishing was originally designed for catching salmonids, or fish of the Salmonidae family. They are intelligent, wily, strong, athletic, and willful animals. In other words, they are not easily taken.

Salmonids are cold-water dwellers, native only to the Northern Hemisphere, although they have been transplanted to cold places in the Southern Hemisphere. They are insectivores, devourers of water-born insects, and fly fishing was once simply about catching them with imitation insects. Now, though, some fly fishers use imitation bait fish, frogs, and mice, as well as loud flashy objects that resemble nothing in nature but are designed to catch a fish's attention. Also it is increasingly popular to fly fish for non-salmonid species, especially in the ocean.

Salmonids are commonly called trout, salmon, and char, but are also known by a few other names. In the North Slope of Alaska and far northern Canada lives a salmonid of the genus *Stenodus*, known to the locals by the French name Inconnu, or "unknown."

From another genus, *Hucho*, comes the taimen, which is the largest salmonid, found in Russia and Mongolia. These giants do not go to sea and yet grow to between thirty and seventy pounds. The largest one ever recorded, caught in the Kotui River in 1943, was eighty-three inches long and weighed ninety-two and a half pounds, though there may have been larger ones unrecorded. Today, the taimen are declining in number and are considered to be an endangered species.

The grayling is a lively trout-like fish from the *Thymallus* genus. I once caught a twenty-two-inch grayling on the Ozernaya in Russia, causing my guide to excitedly exclaim that I had beaten the world record. The fish was actually a few inches short of that, but it was the largest grayling I had ever seen.

The salmonids that are the most valued belong to one of three genera: *Oncorhynchus*, *Salmo*, and *Salvelinus*. Two of these genera include salmon, one includes char, and all three include fish that we call trout. Even the huge taimen, whose genus is totally different from these three, is called a trout. This begs the question, what is a trout? From a scientific point of view, there is no real definition. Trout is not a scientific term. It is a name commonly used for freshwater salmonids distinguished by various spots and stripes of often very different colors and even different markings. Trout are also generally smaller than salmon, except when the taimen is called a trout.

Many believe that the difference between salmon and trout is that salmon go to sea and trout remain in freshwater. But this is not true. There are salmon that never go to sea and quite a few trout that do. Some brown trout go to sea, grow large, and return as salmon-size fish that we call sea trout. Some rainbow trout go to sea and return as pink-fleshed, silver-skinned giants that we call steelheads. Golden, cutthroat, and other western trout also sometimes go to sea, though they usually don't stay for long. Biologists believe that any salmonid that cannot find sufficient nutrition in a river and has access to an ocean might sojourn out into it for short periods.

In the genus *Oncorhynchus* are eight different species of salmon, all of which live only in the Pacific Ocean. Two of them, *masu* and *amago*, are unique to Asia and are so similar that scientists argue about whether they really are two different species. The full name of the *masu* is *sakuramasu*, which means "cherry trout" even though the fish are clearly salmon: the confusion about what is a trout is not unique to the English language. In Japanese they are frequently just called *masu*, which means trout, even though they are easily identifiable as a salmon. The reason they are called cherry is not because they are particularly beautiful, which they are, but because these salmon re-enter the rivers to spawn at the cherry blossom season. They can be found in Russia's Kamchatka peninsula, as can all eight pacific salmon, but also a few in South Korea. But the largest number are found in Japan's northern island Hokkaido. The salmon rivers can be beautiful in the spring with flowering trees on the banks and cherry salmon running in the rivers.

Shirbetsu River, Kimobetsu, Hokkaido, Japan, where cherry salmon spawn

It is not easy to go fly fishing for cherry salmon in Hokkaido. The Japanese have a tradition of fly fishing, but no tradition of providing guides, and the government does not allow cherry salmon fishing in many of Hokkaido's rivers, as they consider the fish to be a national treasure. But there are a few beautiful rivers, like the Shirbetsu with its gravel bottom and deep pools, where cherry salmon fishing is allowed. Overhead towers the stately Mount Yotei, an active volcano that so resembles the famous Mount Fuji that it is sometimes called Ezo Fuju, which means Hokkaido's Mount Fuji. Some cherry salmon also spawn in the rivers of Hokkaido's capital city, Sapporo, which is not the only metropolis where fish spawn. Sockeye spawn in the city of Vancouver, Canada.

The other six salmon of the genus *Oncorhynchus*—which means "hook-nosed," because of the odd shape the male nose develops when the fish is about to spawn—live all over the Pacific Ocean. The fly fishers' favorite is the king fish, sometimes called the Chinook, after a Native American tribe that caught and traded them in the Pacific Northwest before the Europeans arrived. The king is the favorite because it is the biggest of the *Oncorhynchus* species and puts up the toughest fight.

The second-largest fish of the *Oncorhynchus* genus are chums, which are sometimes called dogfish. Although a highly valued species in Asia, commercial and sports fishers in North America tend to sneer at them, perhaps because although they are large and fight almost as hard as the king, they are not nearly as beautiful. The Japanese appreciate chum, however, and have taught the Alaskans to do so, because they produce the best salmon caviar.

Pinks, the most abundant and, evolutionarily speaking, youngest of the *Oncorhynchus* genus, are not particularly valued either. Although fly fishers seldom eat their catch, they tend to follow commercial judgments and are aware that the pink's flesh is considered inferior. Since the mid-nineteenth century, pinks have been harvested primarily to be canned.

The name sockeye is of uncertain origin, but probably from a Native American word—most likely the Salish word *suk-kegh* from the people of British Columbia's lower Fraser River, a word that simply means "red fish." Sockeye are popular with both gourmets and fly fishers and are one of my favorites, too, in part because their deep red flesh is the most flavorful salmon, but also because they fight hard. They like to hide in grassy parts of the river and tend to take the fly very softly before exploding in fury. A sockeye does not relent until seemingly exhausted, at which point I am finally able to reel it in. But then, it seems, the fish sees the landing net, realizes what is about to happen, gets a second charge of energy, and furiously runs out all the line I had managed to bring in. This second eruption usually catches me by surprise and spins my reel handle so hard it whacks my fingertips, which is painful. Then, with grudging admiration, I have to fight to reel the fish back in again.

Fly fishers don't generally like fish that are small and easy to catch, but the coho, the smallest salmon, is an exception. Fly fishers love them. More than other salmon, they like to take flies, and they leap, spin, and almost do cartwheels when they are on a line. Unlike other salmonids, too, they are generally fished in estuaries. Other types of salmon deteriorate slowly, over months, after they leave the ocean and enter the river, but the coho spawns soon after entering and then declines very quickly.

For many fishers, the steelhead, a rainbow trout that went to sea and returned, is another favorite. It's a top choice of mine, too, as are all rainbows. No fish fights harder in its weight class: the strength and energy of a little twelve-inch rainbow is extraordinary. And if you get that from a twelve-incher, imagine what kind of fight you get from a forty-pound steelhead. Rainbows and steelheads are also uncommonly beautiful, their luminescent rainbow sides seen only after you take them from the water.

Historically, steelhead are native only to the western rivers of the United States, but many outside anglers discovered them in the nineteenth century and became passionate about fishing for them. Who doesn't want to conquer the large and the beautiful? It is the curse of the tiger, and of all large and beautiful animals. The British started coming for steelhead in the 1870s, and Rudyard Kipling came in 1889, fishing on the Clackamas River in Oregon. A tributary of Portland's Willamette River, the Clackamas was known for its steelhead runs until the beginning of the twentieth century.

Another Oregon river, the Rogue, was also a favorite destination for nineteenth-century British anglers in search of steelhead. Accustomed to quiet English streams, the British must have viewed the Rogue as a ferocious river of true adventure. From its start in the clear waters near Crater Lake, the Rogue is a temperamental river that alternates between glistening smooth stretches and frothing rapids, wide patches and narrow ones where rock outcroppings force the water to rush harder. Along the Rogue's banks tower high forests filled with cedar, pine, and redwood trees, Spanish moss draping off branches, and dogwoods that blossom in spring. It has the feel of a sealed-off paradise.

Western adventure novelist Zane Grey claimed that the Rogue and the Eel, a major California river that runs through a dark redwood forest, were the only places in the world where steelhead take a fly. But although it is true that the fish in every river are slightly different and what works with a species in one river might not work with the same species in another, there are actually quite a few rivers where steelhead take flies.

Today the Rogue has too many dams and the Eel's waters are being drained off by vineyards, but the two remain among the best rivers for steelhead. In fact, it may still be true, as Zane Grey wrote in 1928, that "the happiest lot of any angler would be to live somewhere along the banks of the Rogue, most beautiful stream of Oregon."

Personally, though, I would prefer to settle on the banks of Idaho's Salmon River.

The journey that the steelhead makes from the mouth of the Columbia River at the Pacific Ocean to the upper Salmon River is more than a thousand miles—one of the longest salmon runs in the world. And it is easy to imagine that by the time the fish get to the Salmon, they are so exhausted that they are easy prey. But salmon are able to adapt to different situations—the reason why the fish are different in every river—and the Salmon River steelhead are tough. They never give up. They have already struggled their way upstream past dams and rapids, shoving their noses against powerful currents, gaining an inch at a time. When you hook a salmon, it often darts in a variety of directions, trying to break away, and may even run right at you. But the Salmon River steelhead will not charge downstream even though that would be their fastest and most powerful maneuver. They have fought too hard to get upstream and will not yield one inch.

THE SECOND IMPORTANT salmonid genus is the *Salvelinus*. These fish have a v-shaped bone in their mouths and their spots are often lighter than those of the *Oncorhynchus* genus. The best-known *Salvelinus* are the char, including the Arctic char and the Greenland char, fish with silver skin and red flesh similar to a salmon's. Char resemble salmon in other ways, too, but there are no true salmon in the *Salvelinus* genus.

Char fishing is not tremendously popular because you can catch other salmonids without going as far north as the char dwell. Farmed char have become very popular, but there is no commercial fishery that harvests wild Arctic char (despite what some stores claim). So if you want to taste one, you have to go to the Arctic and catch it yourself. The rivers of Iceland are a good place to do so, and have become popular with fly fishers. The rivers' banks are flat and volcanic with little plant growth and their bottoms are often very soft from volcanic ash. At first that seems to make the fishing easier, but you have to be careful not to let your boots sink in.

Another *Salvelinus* fish is the Dolly Varden, which is sometimes called a trout and sometimes a char. The fish is named after a character in Charles Dickens's *Barnaby Rudge* whom Dickens described as having "good humor and blooming beauty." I don't really see these qualities in the fish, which seems to me to be a pale and less attractive member of the salmonoid family. The first time I caught one I was excited because I had never caught one before and because I'm always hoping to catch a new salmonid; it is regarded as a badge of honor to have caught more than twelve salmanoid species and I am stuck somewhere around ten. That day I was fishing for sockeye in Alaska and at first I thought that I had caught a sockeye. It didn't seem to be as strong or fight as long as sockeye usually do, however, so next I thought that maybe I had hooked a jack, or a salmon that has returned to spawn when it is too young and small. When it turned out to be a Dolly Varden, my first Dolly Varden, I was pleased, but my guide could not conceal his contempt. The Dolly Varden have no standing in Alaska, where they are regarded as negatively as whitefish are in Idaho.

Somewhere between when an English literature fan named them in the nineteenth century and the early twentieth century, Dolly Varden lost their standing: it was discovered that the Dolly Varden ate the eggs of other salmonids. In 1921 the United States Bureau of Fisheries even offered two to five cents for every Dolly Varden tail. Humans are forever establishing rules of behavior for animals that animals simply ignore.

In any event, Dolly Varden bounty hunting did not last long, because the bounty fishers tried to pass off all kinds of tails, including sockeye and Chinook tails, as coming from the Dolly Varden. The handing out of bounty money ended in 1939, but the Dolly Varden's negative image has lived on.

It was probably true about the Dolly Varden because that is what salmonids do, they eat the eggs of other salmonids—they even eat the eggs of their own species. Bait fishers know this and so they often use salmon eggs as salmon bait, and fly fishers know this and so they often use beads that resemble salmon eggs.

I was once invited to go fishing for Chinook on the Willamette River in Oregon. It was an unusually warm sunny day and it seemed like everyone in Portland who had a boat or knew someone who did was out on the river, baiting hooks with salmon eggs. The eggs did attract the Chinook, but with so many eggs drifting in the river, they also attracted sea lions. Highly intelligent animals, the sea lions could have been happy with the eggs alone, but they quickly realized that Chinooks with big fat bellies (they love the bellies) were arriving, and any time a fisher lifted a landing net, a sea lion darted over to it and grabbed the salmon. The fishers tried to maneuver the nets in a way that would be less noticeable to the sea lions, but those sea lions were paying attention.

The largest fish in the char family is the lake trout, more correctly called a lake char. It has many other names as well, including mackinaw and namaycush, the latter an Algonquin or Cree name that means "dweller of the deep." The lake trout are giants that can weigh as much as one hundred pounds, but fly fishers still go after them. They are native to only a few North American lakes, including some of the Great Lakes, but because of their popularity they have been transplanted to Europe, Asia, and South America. They were illegally introduced to Yellowstone Lake and since Yellowstone Park tries to maintain its natural order, these large hungry foreigners are considered a problem.

Lake trout usually live in deep water in the middle of large lakes. The town of Geneva, New York, on Lake Seneca, holds an annual lake trout–fishing derby for the largest catch, but the lake trout population there is declining. Like many deep-water fish, lake trout grow very slowly and only reproduce late in life. Such fish can easily be overfished since most of the fish that are caught have not yet spawned.

There are numerous other *Salvelinus*, some called char and others trout, among them the blueback trout, Baffin char, Sunapee trout, red trout (popular in Quebec), long-finned char, silver trout, and aurora trout. A bull trout, also a char, seems very much like a Dolly Varden but larger and therefore more popular. It was actually not recognized as a separate species until 1978. From the perspective of fly fishers, though, the most important *Salvelinus* is the brook trout. The native trout of eastern North America, and the only native of many eastern rivers, the brook trout's habitat ranges from northern Canada to Georgia and Alabama.

Like many other salmonids, brook trout are remarkably adaptable. When left in peace in a big river, they will grow into large fish. But when living in the narrow streams from which they derive their name, brookies, as they are often called, remain small, and beautiful, with gold and violet speckles set off by dark backs and bright red bellies.

For fly fishers, brookies are like teenagers. They are a little wild, indiscriminate, and gullible, and lack caution. They are athletic, like to jump, and will sometimes take a fly on the way down from a leap. (Rainbows do the reverse and grab a fly on their way up). Brook trout are not trophy fish—a six-pound brookie is phenomenal—but they are fun, and many people believe that they are the best-tasting of all trout.

To people who live by the Atlantic Ocean, the most important salmonid genus is the *Salmo*, of which there are about forty-five species (some scientists list a few more and some a few less). All but one of them are considered trout. The exception is the Atlantic salmon, *Salmo salar*, for which the genus was named and from which the word *salmon* was invented. The genus also includes the only fish that is scientifically named trout, *Salmo trutta* or brown trout. All other trout are commonly called trout only because they resemble a brown trout.

TROUT AND SALMON, and hence fly fishing, have traveled far beyond their natural geographic range, in part because fly fishers have wanted to fish for them wherever they go. The movement began even before Charles Darwin had fully expressed his theory of evolution in 1859. It was called acclimatization, and the idea behind it was that plants and animals could change, adapt to different climates, meaning that a species from most anywhere could learn to live elsewhere. The first acclimatizing organization, the Société Zoologique d'Acclimatation, was formed in Paris in 1854 and began shipping exotic species such as ostriches and zebras around the French empire.

The movement drew numerous eccentrics. The reason why starlings are now a common American bird is that a New York

City pharmaceutical maker, Eugene Schieffelin, believed that in order to create a culturally sophisticated society, Americans should have every bird mentioned in Shakespeare. In *Henry IV* Part 1, Act 1, Hotspur, furious that the king has forbidden him to speak Mortimer's name, says,

> Nay, I'll have a starling shall be taught to speak
> Nothing but "Mortimer," and give it him
> To keep his anger still in motion.

And that is the inspiration for the American starling. Schieffelin began bringing starlings to Central Park in 1890 and apparently the birds, though they never said Mortimer's name, found America to be culturally or at least ecologically suitable, as starlings now flourish throughout the United States.

Originally, though, acclimatization was an imperialist concept in an age of Empire. All parts of an empire should contain all major plants and creatures, or so it was believed. After the movement started in France, the British took it up, though they often seemed to be less interested in adapting species to other climates than in moving species from the cold Northern Hemisphere to the cold Southern Hemisphere for the pleasure of British sportsmen. Salmonids, for example, were a once uniquely Northern Hemisphere phenomena, but thanks to the British, salmon and trout now frolic in the waters of Australia, New Zealand, South Africa, and Chile. They tried to assure that anywhere a British colonist went, there would be good game for a fly rod.

The British struggled for a long time to transplant the British Atlantic salmon. They wanted *their* salmon to go with them everywhere. Finally, however, the British realized that there were also salmon in the Pacific Ocean. In New Zealand, Atlantic salmon hatcheries struggled until 1905 when it was discovered that the large and appealing California kings, not the Atlantics, prospered in their waters.

Today, the brown trout has a huge geographic range—they almost seem to be the default salmonid. I once caught huge brown trout in the Suðurland River in Iceland (an unfriendly river for trout, without a gravel bottom) while trying to catch Arctic char; and caught strong tough ones in the rushing Roaring Fork in Colorado while trying for rainbow (though neither browns nor rainbows are native to Colorado); and a handsome one in Ireland while trying for Atlantic salmon. A brown trout is never a disappointment. They can be found in most of the clean rivers of Britain and much of Europe, all the way to northern Russia. They are also in Turkey (in the upper waters of the Tigris and Euphrates), Greece, Albania, Lebanon, the Mediterranean, the mountains of Corsica and Sardinia, and even the black, snow-capped Atlas mountains that rise out of the Moroccan desert.

The British, who were spreading out all over the globe, found it unbearable to live by a cold river that did not have brown trout in it. In 1864 the British took brown trout eggs from the River Itchen in Hampshire, one of England's most famous rivers for brown trout, and transplanted them to Tasmania, an island south of the Australian mainland and one of the coldest places in that country. The transplant was a great success and soon thereafter, the British transplanted brown trout to mainland Australia and New Zealand, Canada, the United States, South Africa, the Falkland Islands, and South America.

Browns transplant easily because they are an extremely adaptable fish. I have caught them in a number of American

Suðurland River by volcanoes, Iceland, where arctic char and large brown trout swim

and European rivers, and each time they look very different. At one time, more than fifty brown trout species were recognized, but it has since been concluded that though the brown trout's skin markings vary, they are all very similar and belong to the same species.

Browns do not run to sea everywhere, but in Britain and Scandinavia sea-run browns, salmon-sized fish called sea trout, are a popular fly fishing sport. In the United States brown trout may be the most fly fished trout. They swim with the *Oncorhynchus* in western rivers and with the brookies in the east. Even in New England and upstate New York, fishermen are often happier to catch a brown than a native brook trout. I once heard a fly fisherman in Manchester, Vermont, complain that there were not enough browns and "too many brook trout" in the Battenkill, even though brookies are that river's only native fish.

Although the British were outspoken in their belief that brookies were too easily taken and not up to the standard of the larger, more wily browns, the first trout to be transplanted in the United States were brook trout, moved to California because there were so many transplanted easterners there who missed their native trout. The first browns in the United States were not English but German, a gift from the Black Forest.

Any trout can be easy to catch in some circumstances on some days and extremely difficult to catch on others. A brown trout is also probably a tougher fish to catch in an American river than in an English one. England's famed "chalk streams," so called because of their high lime content, are far gentler than hard-rushing American rivers, and the adaptable trout becomes tougher on rougher rivers. Red Smith said that the brown trout were "invented" on English rivers in "a crude, primitive form," but on the Beaverkill in upstate New York "they painted spots on him and taught him to swim."

Brown trout may be popular, but many anglers, myself included, would rather fish for a rainbow than for any other kind of trout. Theodore Gordon, one of the great nineteenth-century pioneers of American fly fishing, famed for fishing the Beaverkill, wrote: "The rainbow leaps again and again, and always runs downstream (downstream is faster) . . . the rainbow, after throwing into the air, tears desperately down, and you must follow if the fish is any size . . . It fights to the last, and when landed has scarcely a kick left in it."

It is for this reason that rainbows have been transplanted from western to eastern rivers and are now as ubiquitous as browns. Even the brown-loving British wanted rainbows in their rivers, but transplanting them was not successful and only a very few English rivers have rainbows today.

By the 1870s, fishery planners realized that there would be a far greater demand for rainbows in the East than for brookies in the West. In the famous hatchery on the McCloud River in California, Livingston Stone, a Boston native who became a leader in aquaculture, struggled to propagate salmon in the McCloud but had great success with rainbows.

The natural range of rainbows stretches from Mexico to Alaska to the Kamchatka Peninsula in Russia, but they were naturally found in only a few U.S. states, principally California, Oregon, Washington, and Idaho. Today, though, they are found in every U.S. state and in eighty-eight other countries in every continent except Antarctica. Over millennia, sheep, dogs, and other domesticated animals, as well as cultivated grains and other crops, spread around the globe in a similar manner, but the rainbow trout did so in just a hundred years.

Not without negative consequences. In Chile, where rainbows have grown to enormous size, the frog population is declining. Frogs are among the creatures that rainbows love to

Rainbow trout chasing a fly

eat. The invaders have also had a huge impact on the aquatic insect population of the Southern Hemisphere.

Still, everyone loves their rainbows. South Africa has proposed making rainbow trout "an honorary indigenous species," which may seem a bizarre misconception but the rainbow trout was once named the state fish of both Colorado and Utah even though it is not native to either. In the 1990s the mistake was corrected.

FOR FLY FISHERS with international experience, the greatest salmonid to catch on a fly is an Atlantic salmon. This is partly because the Atlantic is the hardest to catch. Zane Grey wrote that Pacific salmon were neither as good fighters nor as beautiful as Atlantic salmon, and even Roderick Haig-Brown, the beloved fishing writer from British Columbia, admitted with reluctance that catching Pacifics was not as good a sport as catching Atlantics. Similarly, Lee Wulff, born in Valdez, Alaska, in the heart of Pacific salmon country, wrote, "Atlantic salmon fishing represents, in all likelihood, the highest development of individual angling known on this continent."

These anglers were being very picky, because catching a Pacific salmon on a fly is an exceptional experience. I suppose their preference for Atlantics is partly because the odds of catching an Atlantic are far slimmer than the odds of catching a Pacific. There are only one and a half million Atlantic salmon left on the planet, which is why, if you do catch one, you have to handle it with great care and put it back in the river. Wulff, who claimed to have caught seventy-five Atlantics on one day in Eastern Canada, meaning that he had to put seventy-five fish back in the river, too, still preferred fishing them to Pacifics.

By the time I caught my first Atlantic, I had already caught numerous Pacifics, which no one had fussed about. But when I caught that one relatively small Atlantic on the River Thurso in the Scottish Highlands, I received numerous emails of congratulations from people I knew all over Scotland. Word travels fast in the Highlands. And catching an Atlantic is an event.

After a salmonid gets hooked by a fly, it suddenly erupts with energy—and so do you. It feels like you are trying to hold a furious wild animal on a string. The fish's strength matches your own. You try to pull it in and it tries to get away. If you pull too hard, the line will break and the fish will be lost. But if there is any slack in the line, the fish can either unhook or snap the leader. So a perfect tension must be maintained.

A wild fish is not just pulling away, it is leaping in the air, running to the left and then the right, trying to break the line by going behind a rock, leaping again and changing directions, all the while trying to get away faster than you can get out the line. And no fish plays this game better than an Atlantic salmon. Salmon do not give up, so every tiny measure of strength in the salmon's athletic body has to be used up before you can pull it in. By then most of your strength may be sapped as well, but you are too excited to realize it.

As fly fishing has grown in popularity, fly fishing techniques have been applied to a variety of other fish species such as bass, bonefish, tarpon, barracuda, tuna, sailfish, and marlin. In 1881, a popular fly fishing writer, James A. Henshall from Ohio, wrote a book on using trout and salmon flies for fishing black bass. Bass, especially large-mouth bass, had endeared themselves to anglers by the sudden ferocity with which they gobbled up flies. Large-mouth bass have the capacity to gulp down bats, birds, frogs, and more, and so can take large and outrageous flies.

Fly fishing for saltwater fish such as bonefish, marlin, and tuna is not new. The Roman Claudius Aelianus wrote of fishing in the ocean with hooks wrapped in wool with a seagull feather. In an 1843 article a British writer said that he had been casting in the ocean for more than forty years. But since saltwater fish do not eat insects, saltwater flies are not really flies. They aren't always flies in rivers either. Trout and saltwater flies often imitate bait fish or shrimp.

Saltwater fishing did not really take off until the second half of the twentieth century, probably because that was when a wide variety of synthetic materials became available. Saltwater flies are always made of synthetic material because it does not absorb water, enabling a large fly to remain lightweight.

Angling for bonefish has a growing number of fans in the Bahamas and Florida. Zane Grey described bonefish as "the wisest, shyest, wariest, strangest fish I have ever studied." Personally, I doubt they are as wise as salmonids, but they are extremely strong and fast. The appeal in catching one lies not so much in getting it to take a fly as in holding on to it once it does.

Fishers catch bonefish on shallow mudflats using flies that imitate the little minnows on which the fish feed. In 1977 a bright yellow fly with beads for eyes named a "Crazy Charlie" became a popular bonefish fly. But the fish has to be tracked down before you can cast because it will only take a fly when the fly has been placed in an appealing position. So a great deal of the time, bonefish fishing is about sloshing through mudflats looking for fish. This is hard going, especially since it is usually done in considerable heat. You have to truly love bonefish fishing to enjoy a day like that.

I have fished barracuda in West Africa and found them to be curious fish who will swim up to have a look at you. If you approach them, they will back up, maintaining the same distance away from you all the while. If you hook a barracuda, you have to handle it carefully because although their jaws are powerful, they are also very delicate.

Anglers desire tarpon, tuna, and marlin mostly because they are large and put up a tough fight. Tarpon and marlin, both tropical fish, are spectacular leapers. Tuna are extremely strong and, unlike the tarpon and marlin, have the misfortune of having extremely delicious flesh. Most people are pleased to throw back their marlin or tarpon, at least after the photo is taken, but they like to keep a good tuna. A yellowfin tuna can weigh well over three hundred pounds and be six feet long, and in the American Atlantic range from Brazil to Massachusetts. They feed on the surface of the water, which makes them highly susceptible to flies. But once the hook is set, the powerful animals that can swim fifty miles per hour will fight against

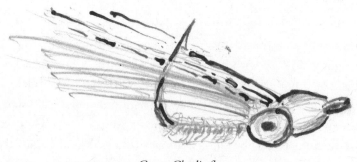

Crazy Charlie fly

being landed for two hours or more. All this has earned them a reputation as one of the great fly targets.

Yet for a purist, despite this variety of saltwater prey, there really is nothing like standing in a cold river trying for a salmonid. Jimmy Carter once wrote, "Although I had fished for bass, bream, catfish and other warm water fish since I was a child, and still enjoy it just as much as ever, there is something special about fly fishing for trout."

Yes, there is.

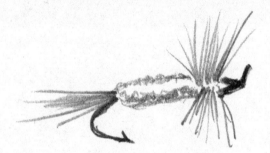

Rat-face Macdougall fly

4

Who Started This?

Let your hook always be cast
In a pool where you least expect it,
There will be a fish.

—OVID, *THE ART OF LOVE, BOOK III*

The above quote from a poem by Ovid is the earliest-
known version of what has become a fly fisher's cliché:
"You can't catch a fish unless your fly is in the water." The poem
was written in the last years of the first century B.C., and it's
surprising to realize how ancient fly fishing is, especially since
it's the most evolved form of fishing, or at least so fly fishers
claim. To understand the history of fly fishing, we have to
rethink the nature of the ancients and possibly fly fishing itself.

We tend to think of the ancients as pragmatists, inventing,
building, securing food supplies, and conquering. And of
course it's very possible that they invented fly fishing as just one
more possible way to catch fish. Few people were exclusively
fly fishers until modern times. The fisher who wouldn't dream

of catching a fish any other way or the river where no other technique is allowed are largely modern responses to the idea that fish are becoming scarce. Originally it was just one of the ways to capture fish.

The ancients also wrote poetry, philosophized, and, especially when it came to the Romans, had an almost fetish-like fascination with food. So, perhaps they could see that there is more to fishing than just catching fish. Judging from some of their writings, they had a great interest in understanding nature, and fly fishing is an attempt to imitate nature: it's almost a study in how nature works.

Historians argue over what was the earliest fishing technique—the net, the spear, or the line. There is supporting evidence for all three.

For thousands of years, fishing was done with a "gorge," which is a piece of flint, bone, shell, or horn, pointed on both ends. Very early humans knew how to entice the fish to swallow the gorge (one of the meanings of the Latin word *gurga*, the origin of *gorge*, is "throat") by putting bait on it. When the line was pulled tight, the gorge turned sideways in the fish's throat. Gorges that are seventy thousand years old, from the Paleolithic period, have been found. Eventually, though, fishers realized that a fish would hold better to a gorge if it was bent, and hooks of every imaginable material started to be made. The Maori made hooks with human bones. The New Guinean people made them with the claws of large insects. Hooks were also made from eagle jaws and barrel cactus spurs. And the ancient Egyptians were the first to realize that a hook would hold even better in a fish's mouth if had a reverse point, a barb, which had already been used on spears.

★　★　★

ACCORDING TO ANCIENT Chinese mythology, the emperor Shennong, who taught humankind the use of fire, invented the plow, and cataloged herbal medicines, also taught people how to tie a line spun from a silkworm cocoon to the end of a thorn stick and put a sharpened piece of iron with split grain for bait on the stick's other end. This is not far off from the fishing method I used as a child.

In a manuscript written about 3,500 years ago, during the Shang Dynasty, which ruled the Yellow River Valley, the use of an artificial fly for fishing was described. I have crossed the wide, rushing, gravel-bottomed Yellow River, which in the spring literally turns yellow because of its mineral content, a number of times and it does look like it might be suitable for fly fishing. Its only drawback is the cloudiness of its water. But were anglers actually fly fishing during the Shang Dynasty?

Confucius wrote of fishing on the Yellow River, but what he described is almost the opposite of fly fishing. His fishermen used a bream for bait, and when that didn't work, switched to half a suckling pig (which half is not specified) and quickly caught a fish "the size of a cart." Confucius apparently believed the common myth that the larger the bait, the larger the fish that is caught with it. Modern fly fishers often make the same mistake.

The first Chinese historical reference to rod-fishing occurs in *The Book of Odes*, written between the eleventh and seventh century B.C. The document mentions bamboo rods, used in China more than twenty centuries before the British "invented" them. The line attached to the bamboo rods was silk thread.

There are ancient Western records, including works by Homer, that also mention fishing with a rod. But it is generally accepted that the earliest record of fly fishing comes from Claudius Aelianus. By the time he was writing, late in the second century and early in the third A.D., fishing with a rod, line, and hook was already well established. He describes Macedonian fishermen in his book *On the Nature of Animals*:

> *I have heard of a Macedonian way of catching fish, and it is this:* between Boroea and Thessalonica runs a river called the Astraeus, and in there are fish with speckled skins . . . These fish feed on a fly peculiar to the country, which hovers on the river. When a fish observes a fly on the surface, it swims quietly up, afraid to disturb the water above, lest it should scare away its prey; then coming up by its shadow, it opens its mouth gently and gulps down the fly, like a wolf carrying off a sheep from the fold or an eagle a goose from the farmyard; having done this it goes below the rippling water.
>
> Now though the fishermen know of this, they do not use these flies at all for bait for fish; for if a man's hand touch them, they lose their natural color. Their wings wither, and they become unfit food for the fish . . .
>
> They fasten red wool round a hook and fix on to the wool two feathers which grow under a cock's wattles, and which in color are like wax. Their rod is six feet long, and their line is the same length. Then they throw their snare, and the fish, attracted and maddened by the color, comes straight at it, thinking from the pretty sight to gain a dainty mouthful; when, however, it opens its jaws, it is caught by the hook, and enjoys a bitter repast, a captive.

This method of fishing may have been new to Aelianus, but it was apparently not new to the Macedonians. Aelianus is known for taking information from other writers, sometimes writers of a century earlier and sometimes writers whose work has been lost, which makes his manuscripts of great value to scholars today.

The Spanish-born Roman poet Martial, writing a century before Aelianus, also made a reference to fly fishing:

> Who has not seen the scarus rise,
> Decoyed and killed by fraudful flies?

The scarus is a Mediterranean parrotfish much appreciated by the Romans, and these lines may be the earliest surviving reference to fly fishing. Here again, though, fly fishing is presented as a well-known activity, not something new, so presumably it was already common.

Plutarch, the great Greek biographer, who might have been a fly fisherman himself, had very sound advice on fishing. He said the rod needed to be thick enough for a large fish but not so thick that its shadow would scare fish. This sounds very much like advice given to fly fishers today. Plutarch also recommended that the line be made of horsehair and have as few knots as possible because the fish could see them. A line made from the tail of a white stallion was best, he claimed, as white stallions had the strongest hair; the tails of mares and geldings had been weakened by urine (this is not true). Plutarch also advised using a rod made of cane, which many fishers today still believe makes the best rods.

AELIANUS'S ACCOUNT HAS two striking elements to it. First, it is an accurate description of fly fishing for trout, as valid today as it was then. And second, the fishermen he describes are not trying to make fishing more challenging or sporting. They are simply using the most practical system there is for catching trout. This argues for the theory that fly fishing was developed for purely practical reasons. Perhaps, as Theodore Gordon, the father of American fly fishing, said, it all simply began when an ancient fisherman saw a trout rising to catch a fly and decided he needed to use flies rather than worms for bait. From there it would not have been a great leap to craft artificial flies rather than capture and tie on real ones.

It would also not be surprising if the Romans had developed fly fishing for practical rather than sporting reasons. Unlike the Greeks and Egyptians, they were not great fishermen. They loved to eat fish, but did not want to expend a great effort to catch one. There is a famous story about Mark Antony and Cleopatra going fishing together. Being Egyptian, Cleopatra was a serious angler. Being Roman, Marc Antony was not, and so arranged for a diver to attach a large fish to his hook so that he could impress the Egyptian. She was not fooled by this slick Roman and arranged for a diver to attach a cured salt fish to Mark Antony's line, and when he hauled it up, everyone laughed at him.

The Romans were always looking for new fishing techniques. They tried dropping half-filled bottles of wine and incense into the water to try to intoxicate fish. They also tried dressing themselves in female goat skins; it had been found that when female goats entered shallow pools to cool off, fish would swarm around them. This idea of fish being attracted to females, including human females, persists to this day among some fishermen.

The Romans also practiced "fish tickling," a fishing technique that was probably in use long before they took it up.

When a fish is seen near the surface of the water, a fisherman gently passes a hand underneath it and strokes its belly, which puts it into a trance. Then he grabs the fish and tosses it to shore. In Shakespeare's *Twelfth Night* there is a reference to trout tickling. Early Americans called it "noodling."

After Aelianus, centuries went by with little mention of fly fishing in Europe, though it is believed that the activity never stopped. The Romans were great chroniclers of their daily lives, but the medieval Europeans were not. There were few literate Europeans even among the aristocracy; reading and writing were principally activities of the church. Not until the end of the fifteenth century did literacy rates in Europe start to climb to 20 percent, though mostly only among male aristocrats.

The oldest-known writing on fishing in England, *The Colloquy of Aelfric*, dates from 995. In this book, a tenth-century abbot named Aelfric, archbishop of Canterbury, known for his writing in Anglo-Saxon, makes clear that fishing is about commerce, not sport. The fisherman in his colloquy states that the purpose of fishing is "food, clothing, and money." He expresses his preference for river fishing over fishing at sea and says of whaling, "I would rather catch a fish I can kill than one that can kill me." He also expresses a distaste for rowing.

Aelfric writes a great deal about the species of fish taken by his fisherman, but unfortunately says little about what fishing technique was used. He writes of both nets and hooks, but when writing of hooks and lines does not make clear whether the fisherman used a rod or a hand line.

Writing on fly fishing appeared in Germany starting in the twelfth century. There are many references to the *vederangel*, a feathered hook used to catch trout and grayling. Commoners in many parts of Germany apparently used this hook from the fourteenth century on, and fished for food or amusement, not commerce. These are some of the earliest known references to the commoner as sports fisherman.

In 1486 the printer Wynkyn de Worde published *The Book of St Albans*. Wynkyn de Worde was an immigrant brought over to England by William Caxton, who had also brought over England's first printing press. Dutch according to some and Alsatian according to others, de Worde was an experienced printer and the founding father of the British printing industry, the first to establish printing on Fleet Street in London. *The Book of St Albans*, named after the abbey where it was compiled, is a compendium of writings on hunting, hawking, and other sports of the fifteenth century.

Included in the book is the unusual *A Treatyse of Fysshyng wyth an Angle*. A guide to fly fishing, it contains information on how to fashion the proper hooks, how to tie flies, including exact instructions for tying twelve flies, and how to cast. It even warns against overfishing. It is a manual on fly fishing that could still be useful today.

Some historians believe that the treatise was written as many as fifty years before it was included in *The Book of St Albans*. A handwritten version of it dating from about 1450 also exists. Both versions seem to be incomplete copies of an original that has been lost.

At first the *Treatyse* was said to have been penned by an anonymous writer, but as the centuries passed, an author was created. Later editions were authored by Dame Juliana Berners or in still later editions, Juliana Barnes.

This was incredible. The news spread that "the first book on fly fishing was written by a woman." And not only a woman, but a nun.

Of course, the treatise was by no means the first book on fly fishing—in fact, much of the information in it seems derivative. But it was the most complete book on the subject up to that date.

The Dame Juliana story grew over time. A century later, a church biographer named John Bale wrote that she had been not only a nun but also an aristocratic nun. He praised her for her deep knowledge of field sports and said, "she was an illustrious female, eminently endowed with superior qualities, both mental and personal." Bale was writing this in 1559. Decades earlier King Henry VIII had closed the monasteries and convents, but now some were being allowed to reopen and the church was in need of heroes. Juliana Barnes filled that need. She was exactly what the church historians were looking for.

Unfortunately, though modern historians have searched and searched, there is no evidence that this woman ever existed. She appears to have been a fabrication, and the real author of the treatise remains unknown—just as he or she was in the beginning.

For a woman to have written a book in the fifteenth century is not impossible. In 1438 Margery Kempe dictated to a scribe the first autobiography of a woman written in English. Even earlier, in 1373, Julian of Norwich wrote of the visions she was having in *Revelations of Divine Love*, the earliest known book by a woman in English. But these books were not about hunting or fishing, and though the male clergy often wrote about field sports, it is unlikely that a nun wrote about fly fishing. There is no mention of women in the *Treatyse*, though there are constant references to men, and no indication at all that women fly fished or that the author wanted to encourage it. Most historians find it extremely unlikely that this book was written by a woman.

The *Treatyse* is still being erroneously referred to as the first book on fly fishing and is still often credited to Dame Juliana. Books on women fly fishers often claim that fly fishing started with her. It is a shining illustration of the old newspaper adage, "Don't let the facts ruin a good story." Joan Wulff's book on women fly fishers reprints the entire *Treatyse* and includes an illustration of a nun fly fishing in a medieval habit. Wulff even makes a weak argument that the book had to have been written by a woman because only a woman would advise keeping maggots for bait "under your gown or other warm thing." Wulff writes, "No man would say this would he?" To which I counter, take a look at fifteenth-century clothing.

The *Treatyse* seems to have a different attitude than the other parts of the St Albans collection. It tells us that in the fifteenth and sixteenth centuries, fly fishing was a familiar and popular amusement in England. The other sports described in *The Book of St Albans* appear to be the pastimes of aristocrats, but the *Treatyse* does not seem to have been written exclusively for the wealthy. Its author writes, "The game of angling is profitable to a man for it shall make him rich." With the exception of the owners of certain exclusive fly fishing lodges, I don't know that this has ever been true. Also, the collection's sections on heraldry, hawking, hunting, and the other sports were written in the Norman French language, which became the official language of England after 1066 and was still the language of the court in the fifteenth century, but the *Treatyse* was written in working-class English.

Typeset books were still an exciting novelty and to have one on fly fishing greatly elevated the sport's status in England. The book itself became the written authority on fly fishing for at least the next two centuries and was highly regarded into the nineteenth. The fly-tying patterns it described dominated English fly fishing into the seventeenth century and are still considered important.

But the *Treatyse* was only one of a number of books on fly fishing written in the fifteenth century. This was the age of Johannes Gutenberg and the beginning of book printing. The first printed book on fly fishing, as well as the first known fly fishing book written on the European continent, was printed in Heidelberg in 1493. Also by an anonymous author and also mostly a how-to manual, it is a compendium of various pieces, some by known writers of the era. The book recommends using toxins for catching fish, as well as bait, and concludes that you can catch a lot more fish with toxins than with bait. Also surviving from the fifteenth century is a handwritten codex from a Bavarian abbey in Tegernsee, which includes instructions on how to tie artificial flies made with silk.

Fifteenth- and sixteenth-century fly fishers used rods and lines that were far more difficult to work with in the face of strong winds and other difficult circumstances than the tackle we use today. But these fishers were highly skilled. Their rods were tapered, their hooks were made of strong materials, and they used both sinking and floating flies, depending on the situation they faced.

The writers of the *Treatyse* and other early fly fishing works claimed to have done research before writing their books, implying that there were other fly fishing books that have been lost. Some of these were discovered in the twentieth century.

In 1954, a 1577 British book, *The Arte of Angling*, was found in the attic of an English country home. In 1980, a Belgian historian, W. L. Braekman, uncovered numerous forgotten fourteenth- and fifteenth-century manuscripts on fly fishing in British archives. So, the *Treatyse* was not the first book on fly fishing, but one of several, a part of a growing trend in England. Fly fishing must have been becoming more popular.

More recently, Maggs Brothers, a London rare book dealer, discovered an Austrian manuscript on fly fishing, *The Haslinger Breviary*. Dating back to 1460, the book is now at the Beinecke Rare Book and Manuscript Library at Yale University. Its author, Leonardus Haslinger, an Austrian clergyman, may have originally set out to write a traditional breviary, or clergymen's prayer book, as its right-hand pages are in Latin, written in black and red ink in the ornate hand of a scribe. But its left-hand pages were left blank and have been filled in by a less professional hand, writing in Old German and describing fly patterns. Reading them, it is interesting to imagine what Haslinger was like, compulsively sticking fishing information in his prayer book. Was he contemplating fishing when his mind was supposed to be elsewhere? He apparently did not write his notes just for himself. His instructions on how to tie flies are detailed and substantial and might predate the patterns described in the *Treatyse*. He includes twenty-one fly patterns, sorted according to appropriate months, as well as instructions on how to make hooks.

As fly fishing grew in popularity in Europe, an increasing number of books on the subject emerged. Among them, and coming out of a European tradition of books on hunting, was *The Little Treatise on Fishing* by Fernando Basurto, published in Zaragoza, Spain, in 1539. Hunting books frequently took the form of a dialogue, and this book contains the first dialogue involving a fisherman. In fact, the book is a discussion between a fisherman and a hunter about which sport is better, with the fisherman arguing that fishing is morally superior. Later, when this debate was taken up by the English, writers argued that fishing is safer, more relaxing, and more peaceful than hunting.

Basurto's dialogue gives detailed instructions on fly fishing. He recommends making flies' bodies out of wrapped silk threads (unlike the *Treatyse*, which recommends using heavier wool threads, in patterns similar to those of Aelianus), and using feathers for hackles and wings. He does not specify which feathers to use or how to attach them. He also gives sound casting advice, suggesting that a fisher throw a cast upstream and let the fly drift downstream because he had observed trout feeding on insects in downstream drifts. This is how modern fly fishers generally work as well.

By this time in history, the nature of an artificial fly was clearly established. It was to look like a real insect, with the shaft of the hook concealed in its wrapped body. Attached were wings, usually made of feathers, and hackles made of feather fibers or fur that stuck out from the fly, imitating legs. Later on, other parts of the fly, such as a tail, were also added.

By the 1600s the number of works on fly fishing and probably the number of fly fishers increased. Many of the figures we know from the Elizabethan period were fly fishermen, among them Sir Francis Bacon, who, perhaps not coincidentally, also developed the scientific method. Playwright and poet Ben Jonson was a fly fisherman, and so was Alexander Nowell, an Anglican minister and the dean of St. Paul's Cathedral in London. Nowell was said to have devoted one tenth of his time to fly fishing and gave his fish to the poor—an appealing form of tithing. In 1598 Thomas Bastard, a clergyman given to epigrams and revealing sex scandals, was apparently concerned about overfishing. He wrote of fly fishing;

> But now the sport is marred, and wot ye why?
> Fishes decrease and fishers multiply.

A year after his death in 1589, English author Leonard Mascall's book about fishing for sport, *A Booke of Fishing with Hooke & Line*, was published. He is sometimes credited with introducing carp to England, but this is not true. Carp were brought to England before him. Mascall also authored numerous books on such subjects as fruit orchards, animal traps, cattle, and medicine. Most of these books are of a practical nature, but his fishing book is simply about having fun.

Prominent Elizabethan poet, playwright, and writer Gervase Markham wrote about many subjects, including farming, cooking, and fly fishing, He gave instructions for several fly fish tying patterns that he claimed would create perfect imitations of aquatic insects, and he was one of the first to point out that fish had good vision. Fly fishers needed to dress so that the fish could not easily spot them, he said.

The only piece of writing we know of by John Dennys was the first lengthy poem in English on fishing, *The Secrets of Angling*. The poem is about fishing on the River Boyd, a tributary of the Avon, "in whose fayr streams the speckled Trout doth play." More a bait fisher than a fly fisher, Dennys gives detailed descriptions of fishing. He was a serious fisherman who painted his rod a dark color so the fish couldn't see it and, similar to Markham, suggested that fishermen wear dull-colored clothes to hide from the fish's sharp eyes. "Let your garments russet be or grey," he wrote. The poem is written in 151 verses, eight lines each, and was first published in 1613, four years after Dennys's death. The book became well known, and by 1652, there were four more editions.

Among those influenced by Dennys's poem was writer Isaak Walton, author of the famous *The Compleat Angler: or, the Contemplative Man's Recreation*, published in 1653. A highly derivative work, the book drew upon the previously mentioned 1577 book called *The Arte of Angling*, which itself may have drawn upon the still earlier *Little Treatise on Fishing* by Basurto. *The Arte of Angling* is a dialogue between Piscator the fisherman and Venator the hunter. A nice touch is the inclusion of Cisley, Piscator's wife, who periodically interrupts the dialogue to belittle her husband's hobby.

Like the earlier works, *The Compleat Angler* is a dialogue about fishing, though also included in it is a sometimes disjointed compendium of three dozen poems and songs, one with music included, and many little anecdotes, some resembling jokes. Annoyingly, most of the poems are not about fishing. Why, for example, does Walton include a poem about milkmaids that is a spoof on a John Donne takeoff on a Christopher Marlowe love poem? What do milkmaids have to do with fly fishing? I ask, and many other anglers ask the same.

There is a dialogue between Piscator and Venator on the merits of fishing. While on a fishing trip in the valley of the River Lea, an easygoing chalk stream that flows off of the Thames in East London, they talk about how John Donne, Montaigne, and George Herbert were all fly fishermen, and quote from their works. They also point out that Peter, Paul, and John of the New Testament were fishermen.

"Izaak Walton teaching his scholar how to land a fish—"

Louis Rhead (American, 1857–1926), Izaak Walton teaching his scholar how to land a fish

Though completely unoriginal and often disliked by fly fishermen, *The Compleat Angler* is still published and remains one of the most-published books in the history of English literature. Only the Bible, *The Book of Common Prayer*, and Shakespeare have been reprinted in more editions. How is this possible? It is one of those inexplicable things, like curling becoming an Olympic sport. While readers continue to express disappointment in Walton's work, the book continues to be published and sold. Some suspect that it adorns bookshelves but is seldom read.

Despite the book's longevity and many editions, there has only been one critical study of it or its author by Jonquil Bevan, an English professor at the University of Edinburgh, who also edited the Oxford University Press's 1983 edition of Walton's book. In her study, *The Compleat Angler: The Art of Recreation*, Bevan puzzles over the lack of academic interest in Walton. As one of his greatest fans, she calls his work "a book of great charm" though she admits "that charm is due to its apparent artlessness." She may be right in admiring the book for its literary merits because, despite its oddness, it does occupy a certain space in English literature. Walton lived at a time when England was becoming the dominant country for both fly fishing and fly fishing literature—it was a kind of golden age for fly fishing—and many writers who came after Walton copied him.

The first edition of *The Compleat Angler* was not a deluxe book. It was bound in sheepskin, a material used for less expensive books. Running through it, however, were high-quality engraved illustrations of various fish species. The artist is unknown, but he was clearly a highly skilled copper engraver, and four more of his illustrations were added to the 1655 edition. In the introduction to a nineteenth-century edition of the book, the New England poet James Russell Lowell suggested that if you do not enjoy the book's text, you could always appreciate its pictures. Lowell, a leading poet of his day, also described Walton as a "club footed poet."

Walton successfully climbed the ladder of Elizabethan London society. Born in Stafford in 1593, he was of working-class origin and worked as a tailor. He married a woman whose brother, a wealthy draper, had risen to be a freeman and citizen of London through the Ironmongers, a guild of various labor groups. Through this brother-in-law, Walton, too, became a freeman and citizen of London—a very respectable position. Drawn to poetry, he managed to become an intimate of several great poets, including John Donne. Walton's rise in society was very unusual for his time and place. In Boswell's *Life of Johnson*, Dr. Samuel Johnson is quoted as saying, "It was wonderful that Walton, who was in a very low situation in life, should have been familiarly received by so many great men, and that at a time when the ranks of society were kept more separate than they are now."

Walton first earned his writing reputation as a biographer. Biography at the time was still under the strong influence of Plutarch, the first-century-A.D. Greco-Roman, but Walton took a more innovative approach. In his 1640 biography of John Donne, the first ever written, he included primary material such as Donne's letters, an unusual addition at the time. He also took the liberty of reconstructing conversations. His biographies were therefore much more lively and human than readers of that era had come to expect. Walton's biographies, and especially the one of Donne, were the mainstay of his rising literary reputation. Most of his works were about leading Anglicans (Donne was not only a poet but also the deeply religious dean of St. Paul's Cathedral), and through them, he was also writing a history of the seventeenth-century Anglican Church.

He could not have chosen a worse century in which to do so. On January 30, 1649, a civil war between the Royalists, supporters of the monarchy, and the Puritans, led by Oliver

Cromwell, culminated in the beheading of King Charles I. Afterward, Puritan rule became extremely repressive. Anglican religious rites, such as reading *The Book of Common Prayer*, were not allowed even in the privacy of homes, and the penalties for harboring an Anglican priest were severe. Anglican priests went underground and communicated in code. A writer authoring biographies of notable Anglicans could have been imprisoned.

This is when Walton decided to take up writing about fly fishing. It is not certain how avid a fly fisherman he really was. Some have even suggested that the "Angler" of his fly fishing book's title was really a reference to "Anglican" and that the book's indecipherable hodgepodge of unrelated items somehow hid subversive messages for Anglicans. If so, Walton never revealed it, not even after 1660 when the monarchy was restored.

When *The Compleat Angler* was published in 1653, Walton, age sixty, presented himself not as a political activist, but as an amiable tailor turned poet. Cromwell had just forced his way into Parliament and closed it. Times were even worse for Royalists in 1655 when Walton wrote the first revision of his fishing book. After the Restoration, however, he returned to his biographies, while also periodically revising or enlarging *The Compleat Angler*, which, to his surprise, was becoming a classic.

It has been suggested that Walton was neither a particularly skilled nor knowledgeable fly fisherman. However, if the book is examined carefully, a few true insights can be found. Walton was one of the first to understand that a salmon returns to the river of its birth, so that the full-size salmon in a river are the grown versions of the ones that left as small fish. This was an important insight, though how Walton reached it is unclear. He said he tied ribbons onto the tails of kelts, salmon that survive spawning and return to sea, to test whether they again go back to the river to spawn again. In fact they do, but this test seems improbable because it is doubtful that a ribbon on a salmon's tail would survive in the North Atlantic for a year or more.

Walton may not have been a skilled fly fisherman, but he clearly was a bait fisherman. He writes of fishing with maggots, minnows, worms, grubs, grasshoppers, and even frogs. There was an enormous list of bait to be used for fishing and some suggestions got strange or distasteful. Some were upset with Walton's description of running hooks through live frogs. Bait fishing was probably more popular than fly fishing during his lifetime, and fly fishers certainly were not disdainful of it, as they often are today, when it is sometimes regarded as cheating.

During the seventeenth century, some fishers tried to attract fish with peculiar pastes. A 1681 book by James Chetham, *The Angler's Vade Mecum*, suggested using a paste made of human fat, cat fat, and cumin seeds. Another writer suggested making a paste from the ground dust of a human skull, attainable by robbing graves. And then there was the mention of using young puppies to attract pike, but fortunately dogs have always been more beloved in England than even fishing.

Other fly fishing books included recipes. Thomas Barker, a friend of Walton and a celebrated chef known for his trout specialties, wrote a 1651 book on fly fishing, *The Art of Angling: Wherein are Discovered Many Rare Secrets, Very Necessary to be Knowne by All That Delight in That Recreation*. Despite its lengthy title, the book was only sixteen pages long. In it, Barker offered some advice on both bait- and fly fishing, and gave recipes for

English, French, and Italian stewed trout. This is the English stew, which with a few changes to contemporary equipment remains an excellent dish (still grill on charcoal if you can):

> He broyleth first upon a Charcoale fire; the first thing that you must have a care of is when your Grid-iron is hot you must cool it with ruff Suet, then the skin of your Fish will not break, with care of turning them: when they are nigh broiled take them off of the Grid-iron; set on a Chafing-dish of coals in a stew-Pan or Dish; put in a good quantity of fresh Butter, so much Vinegar as will give the relish, a penny worth of beaten Cinnamon; then put in your broyled fish, and let them stew about halfe an hour will be sufficient, being turned: adorn your Dish with Sippetts [croutons], take the fish out of the Stew-pan, lay them for the service, be sure to squeeze a Lemmon on them: I will warrant them good victuall.

Barker is one of the few cooks, then and now, to offer recipes for trout. This is because trout is not a commercial fish. It cannot be purchased in most fish markets; wild trout are usually available only to fishers. But often certain salmon recipes can be made with trout as well. Here is one example from Robert May, another of Walton's friends. A French-trained English cook, May wrote *The Accomplisht Cook* in 1660, during the Cromwell Interregnum, and revised it in 1685, after the Restoration. Like Walton, and in contrast to Barker, May was a Royalist, so while Barker cooked for Cromwell, May cooked for the Catholics and Royalists. Here is his recipe for a stew, which he said could be made with either a small salmon or a trout:

Take a salmon, draw it, scotch the back, and boil it whole in a stew pan with white wine, put to it also some whole cloves, large mace, slic'd ginger, a bay leaf or two, a bundle of sweet herbs well and hard bound up, some whole pepper, salt, some butter, and vinegar, and an orange in halves; Stew all together and having been well stewed, dish them in a clean scoured dish with carved sippers, lay on the spices and sliced lemon, and run it over with beaten butter, some of the gravy it was stewed in, garnish the dish with some fine searsed [passed through a sieved] manchet [white bread] or searsed ginger.

Walton also had other writer-fisherman friends on both sides of the Cromwell–Royalist divide. Most notable among them were Robert Venables, a soldier who fought under Cromwell, and Charles Cotton, a fellow Royalist. When Walton wrote to Venables in 1663, he said that he had been fishing for only thirty years, which would mean that he took it up when he was nearly forty.

Venables served in Cromwell's campaign to take Ireland, and while there apparently became an expert salmon fly fisherman and one of the first to write about the practice in detail. He was among the first to describe the attention-catching salmon fly as distinct from the small realistic trout fly: "The salmon delights in the most gaudy and orient feathers you can find . . . with long tails and wings." He also suggested tying the fly to a double hook, which is exactly what salmon fly fishers do today, and offered detailed casting advice. His 1662 book, *The Experienced Angler, or Angling improved, being a general discourse of angling, imparting many of the aptest wayes and choicest experiments for the taking of most sorts of fish in pond or river*, would probably be of far greater use today than Walton's book, and yet it has not endured in the same way.

Walton endorsed Venables's book in the highest terms, writing, "I have read and practiced by many books of this kind. Yet I could never find in them that height of judgment and reason which you have manifested in this." Walton was a modest and generous man, not given to envy, one of the reasons why he was so well-liked.

Walton's other close friend, Charles Cotton, was thirty-seven years younger than he and already recognized as a poet, a better poet than Walton, and the more skilled fisherman of the two. The men fished together on the River Dove and spent hours chatting in the little house that Cotton had built on the gentle river. Like Venables and Walton, Cotton sometimes fished with bait but clearly had a passion for fly fishing.

Cotton and Venables were opposites in many ways, not just politically, but also when fishing. Venables fished for salmon in rushing Irish rivers while Cotton fished for trout in gentle English rivers.

Cotton offered advice on casting, saying that it is better to carefully cast upstream rather than just toss in a fly, and suggested fishing from a distance with thin line. He gave instructions for the tying of sixty flies, all of which, he insisted, were realistic imitations of living insects. Cotton had a great affection for Walton, whom he called "father Walton," and for the last edition of *The Compleat Angler* published in Walton's lifetime (in 1676), wrote an additional section on fly fishing.

It is Charles Cotton's addition, *Being Instructions How to Angle for a Trout or Grayling in a Clear Stream*, that gives Walton's book any claim it has to being a useful fly fishing manual. Cotton contributed twelve new chapters, pumped out in ten days to meet a printing deadline, and his work, not Walton's, earns positive reviews from modern fly fishers. Roderick Haig-Brown called Cotton's advice "clear and practical" and wrote, "most of it is sound even today." Haig-Brown considered Cotton the true "father of fly fishing." A pleasant, good-humored man who lost his family fortune to mounting debt that he also inherited, Haig-Brown never stopped drinking and laughing, and he once said, "I cannot think of a man I would rather have known as a friend than Cotton. He was a writer's writer and a fisherman's fisherman."

THE PROBLEM WITH such a long shelf life is that for all Walton's fans, he has had many critics, such as Lord Byron, though Byron's attack seems to be more of a general condemnation of the cruelty of fishing.

> And Angling too, that solitary vice,
> Whatever Isaac Walton sings or says;
> The quaint old cruel coxcomb in his gullet
> Should have a hook and a small trout to pull it.

Fishermen have always been Walton's harshest critics. Richard Franck, a Cromwell veteran who probably had little sympathy for Anglican authors, was one of the first Englishmen to fly fish in Scotland. In his 1694 *Northern Memoires*, he advised fishermen to learn from experience and suggested that Walton had none. He wrote that Walton "stuffed his book with morals from Dubravius and others, not giving one precedent from his own practical experience."

It is hard for an experienced fisherman not to feel this way about the book. The attitude that most resonates with me, the one expressed by most fly fishermen I know, was well expressed by one of the characters in Norman Maclean's *A River Runs Through It*. Two brothers grew up fishing the Big Blackfoot River in Montana, a cold, fast-running river with rock-bound banks, falls, and rapids and deep pools for trout. It is so different from fishing an English chalk stream like the Lea or the Dove that it is barely the same sport. One of the brothers says, "Who ever saw a dairymaid on the Big Blackfoot River?"

"I would like to get him for a day's fishing on Big Blackfoot—with a bet on the side."

I'M NOT SURE how many people still actually read *The Compleat Angler*, but it still sells and people love to browse through it for favorite quotes. Herbert Hoover declared that every fisherman has a favorite Walton quote. His was "We may say of angling, as Dr. Boteler said of strawberries: "Doubtless God could have made a better berry but doubtless God never did and so, if I might be judge, God never did make a more calm, quiet, innocent recreation than angling."

This quote, which really says nothing at all, illustrates my problem with Walton. Jimmy Carter's favorite Walton quote is better:

> Men that are taken to be grave, because nature hath made
> them of a sour complexion; money getting men, men that

spend all their time, first in getting, and next in anxious care to keep it; men that are condemned to be rich, and then always busy or discontented; for these poor rich men, we Anglers pity them perfectly, and stand in no need to borrow their thought to think ourselves so happy. No, no sir, we enjoy a contentedness above the reach of such dispositions.

Being no Walton fan, I thought I would never have a favorite Walton quote, but then, to my surprise, I stumbled across one little pearl. And this is the special thing about Walton—buried in his messy book, if you rake up the bottom, are a few pearls. My favorite quote is when Piscator says, "Nay the trout is not lost, for pray take notice no man can lose what he never had."

FOR CENTURIES, THE English not only dominated fly fishing literature but fly fishing itself. They elevated trout and salmon fishing above all other kinds of fishing, and did not remain contented with their quiet chalk streams for long. Rather, they (and especially the English aristocracy) began searching for wilder rivers, first in Scotland, then in Ireland, and then in Norway.

It was the Cromwellian soldiers, Venables in Ireland and Franck in Scotland, who started taking English fly fishermen farther afield, and the practice continued into the Victorian era. The royal family owned property along the River Dee in Scotland and King George V, who had fished in Norway when younger, became a devotee of fly fishing the Dee. The Queen Mother, Queen Elizabeth, Prince Philip, Prince

Charles, and most of the royal family have all been fishing in Scotland.

Fly fishing for salmon and trout has long been a Scottish tradition as well. Early Scottish cookbooks gave recipes for both fish. Elizabeth Cleland's 1755 *New and Easy Method of Cookery*, the second cookbook ever published in Scotland, contains four trout recipes: trout stewed, potted, and soused, and trout pie. Here is her recipe for trout pie. It speaks only of cutting off the fish's head and fins, but presumably the gutting and scaling has already been done. I would cut off the tail as well and might consider filleting the fish, too, though the bones, which are very healthy, would soften in cooking.

> Cut off the Fins and Heads, season them [fish] with black and Jamaica pepper [allspice], Mace and Salt, put some butter in the bottom of your dish, then your Trouts; put

River Dee, Scotland, Atlantic salmon river

Gravvy and a little claret in it. Cover it with puff paste.
When the paste is cooked they are enough.

IN THE EARLY nineteenth century, Sir Hyde Parker, the eighth
baronet from a family of British admirals, began fly fishing in
Sweden and then in 1828, turned to the River Alta in Norway.
This wide river in the country's far north has been famous
among British salmon fishers ever since. It is an example of
the adage that big fish are found in big rivers. Alta salmon are
sometimes fifty pounds or more, making them the largest
Atlantic salmon in the world.

Sir Hyde Parker and other wealthy English next branched
out to fish Norway's other big northern rivers, the Namsen
and the Tana. The Norwegians called these visiting aristocrats
"the Lords." They arrived on long yachts and purchased local
carriages, which they outfitted with their own harnesses and
staffed with their own coachmen. They worked with local
fishing guides with whom they shared no common language.

The Lords were far from conservationists. They would land,
catch, eat, and throw away enormous quantities. In 1837
William Belton fished the Namsen and caught 1,172 pounds
of salmon in thirty days. Tales such as this brought more Lords
in their yachts. Frequently men and women would fly fish
together. The water was cold and there were no waders, so the
fishing was done from a boat or riverbank.

The best story I know of the English fishing the Alta was
told by novelist Thomas McGuane in his book on fly fishing,
The Longest Silence. McGuane met an Englishman in Norway
who told him a story about his mother. She had had no interest

in fishing, but one day his father convinced her to fish the Alta. She caught a fifty-pound salmon, and then never fished again. Years later, the son sat beside her on her deathbed and as she lay dying, slipping in and out of consciousness, she opened her eyes, looked at him, and said, "You'll never catch a fifty-pound salmon." Then she closed her eyes and died.

Norwegian farmers living along the northern rivers owned commercial netting rights and soon realized that there was more profit to be made in leasing the rivers to the Lords than to commercial fishermen. The Lords also paid handsome fees for guides and built multiroom mansions to live in while they were fly fishing. They furnished these mansions in a dark and plush English style, and decorated their walls with drawings of their catches. The Lords were only in Norway for a few months of the year and often gave the local Norwegians permission to use their mansions when they were gone. Some of these homes have since been abandoned, but others are still occupied by Norwegians and are still decorated with nineteenth-century fly fishing tackle.

At about the same time English fly fishers started leasing rivers in Norway, they also traveled all over the world to catch fish on a fly. Local anglers soon took up the sport, too. Scandinavians, Australians, New Zealanders, and many more—all became fly fishers because of the English.

For a time, fly fishing seemed to be almost mandatory for British public officials. William Gladstone and Neville Chamberlain were dedicated fly fishers, and the popularity of fly fishing in Britain grew even more spectacularly after World War Two. Government income from fishing licenses in England and Wales more than doubled between 1949 and 1959.

Later in the twentieth century, however, in places where the English aristocrats had once dominated, wealthy Americans took over. In 1964 a wealthy American leased the entire Alta River from June 24 to July 24 for $35,000 (the equivalent of $280,000 today). The irony is that it was the English who invented American fly fishing.

Big boy fly

5

American Fly Fishing

What is a matter of a few-million dollars profit compared with landing a ten-pound pickerel!

—ANDREW CARNEGIE, WHEN INTERVIEWED ABOUT A
SUCCESSFUL STEEL DEAL HE HAD JUST NEGOTIATED

Hell, if I had jumped on all the dames I'm supposed to have jumped on, I'd have had no time to go fishing.

—CLARK GABLE, QUOTED BY HOAGY B. CARMICHAEL

The earliest record of fishing with an artificial fly in America comes from the Carolinas. According to one version of the tale, the Native Americans there fished with a fly made from the skin of a deer's leg, cured and with the hairs still on it. The skin was wrapped around the shank of a hook with the hairs pointing outward. When the fly was pulled against the current, the hairs stiffened like hackles, creating movement that attracted fish. The hook was made either of bone or hammered copper.

The practice was recorded by William Bartram, the naturalist son of a leading naturalist. His book, *Travels through North and South Carolina, Georgia, East and West Florida*, published in 1791, is one of the earliest and most famous documents on Native American life. He traveled throughout the Southeast in the 1760s, visiting the Seminoles, Creek, Cherokees, and Choctaws, and observed them fishing for what he said were trout, though it is suspected, given the area, that the quarry were really largemouth bass.

Here is Bartram's description of what he saw:

> [The fish] are taken with hook and line but without any bait. Two people are sitting in a little canoe, one sitting in the stern to steer, and the other near the bow, having a rod ten or twelve feet in length, to one end of which is tied a strong line, about twenty inches in length. To which is fastened three large hooks, back to back. These are fastened very securely, and covered with white hair of a deer's tail, shreds of a red garter, and some particolored feathers all which form a tuft or tassel nearly as large as one's fist. And entirely cover and conceal the hooks this is called a bob. The steersman paddles softly and proceeds slowly along the shore, keeping parallel to it, at a distance just sufficient to admit the fisherman to reach the edge of the floating weeds along shore he now ingeniously swings the bob backwards and forwards, just above the surface, and some times tips the water with it, when the unfortunate cheated trout instantly springs under the weeds and seizes the prey.

It is a great story, a bit like the tale of the nun who started fly fishing in England and almost as unlikely. But unlike Dame Juliana, these fishermen really did exist.

Native Americans were already fishing with lines and from canoes well before the Europeans arrived, but their use of flies probably began with the Europeans. There are no records, drawings, or even legends of fly fishing before then, and it is likely that the Native Americans learned the technique from the English. Their fishing style as described by Bartram has a great deal in common with English fly fishing.

Still, there is some doubt about the matter. Perhaps Native Americans were the world's first fly fishers and their method was only enhanced by contact with the Europeans. A number of flies were adapted from Native American ideas and they did sometimes use artificial lures. The issue is unresolved, but it does seem that even if the Indians were fly fishers, the European Americans did not learn the technique from them.

Most historians believe that the first fly fishermen in America were the English, who arrived on the continent 150 years before Bartram made his observations. In the beginning, though, the English were simply fishing for food. In 1612 Alexander Whitaker of the Virginia Company, the man said to have baptized Pocahontas, wrote home of the wealth of fish to be found in the southern rivers, caught by the colonists with nets.

One of the first American fly fishermen may have been Richard Franck, the Cromwellian veteran turned fishing authority. He was a rigid man with stern, fixed religious and political beliefs—in short, not the type of personality that Walton or Hoover would have predicted would be drawn to angling. But though perhaps an embarrassment to "the

fraternity," Franck was a passionate fly fisherman with exper-
tise and experience far surpassing Walton's. He fly fished
wherever he went and there is strong evidence that he came to
America. Life in England would have been difficult for him
after Cromwell's death in 1658.

Historians believe that Franck arrived in America sometime
after Cromwell's death, but no later than 1680. His awkwardly
titled *A Philosophical Treatise of the Original and Production of
Things; Writ in America in a Time of Solitude* was published in
London in 1687, and his book *The Admirable and Indefatigable
Adventures of the Nine Pious Pilgrims: Written in America in a Time
of Solitude and Divine Contemplation* was published in London
in 1708, the year of his death. Both books show a considerable
familiarity with seventeenth-century America life, and it is
likely that he went fly fishing there.

The second documented American fly fisher, though
perhaps there were numerous others before him, may have been
Richard Brookes, a naturalist and respected medical authority.
Between 1721 and 1763, he wrote or translated numerous
widely read books on medicine and nature, perhaps none as
popular as his fly fishing book, *The Art of Angling*. Ten editions
were published between 1740 and 1800. In the second half of
the eighteenth century Brookes was more widely read than
Walton.

The Art of Angling says nothing about fishing in America,
but Brookes's 1763 book, *A New and Accurate System of Natural
History*, shows that at some point before 1763 he was in America,
and it is likely that he fly fished while there.

North American fly fishing appears to have first taken hold
in the mid-eighteenth century when the British gradually over-
took the French in Quebec. British army officers began spending

their free time fly fishing the great salmon rivers of Quebec and the Maritimes.

British army officer Sir William Johnson may have been among the first to fly fish in the future United States. The British superintendent of Indian Affairs, he lived in the Adirondacks and by 1770 was said to have gone fly fishing near his home on Sacandaga Lake, though it is not known for certain that he used flies.

In 1766 Sir Joseph Banks, later famous for the discoveries he made while sailing with Captain James Cook, was a naturalist aboard a military ship in Newfoundland charged with protecting Britain's cod-fishing stations. It was common practice to take a scientist along on such expeditions. In his diary of the voyage, which was not published until 1971, Banks writes of fly fishing for trout in Labrador and Newfoundland, then among the most remote places on earth.

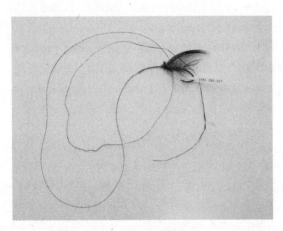

Peter O'Halleran, fly from the J. R. Harris Collection, 1791. Dubbing, goose feather, and hackle tied on a strand of plant material, most likely a now-extinct species of grass.

By the early nineteenth century, fly fishing was well established in Atlantic Canada. The forced exile of numerous pro-
British Loyalists to Canada after the American Revolution
probably helped.

From the beginning, fly fishing in America was about recreation, and the sport always drew more affluent Americans
from population centers such as Philadelphia than rugged
pioneers from the wilderness. Captain John Smith, writing in
1616, viewed rod fishing as recreation, writing of the recently
named "New England," "And what sport doth yield a more
pleasing content and less hurt and change than angling with
a hooke."

New Yorkers were among the first American sports fishers.
The city's early European settlers fished the Collect, a large
body of water in lower Manhattan that in time was destroyed
by New York's twin vices, pollution and real estate development. Thereafter, New Yorkers started traveling ever farther
outside the city to fish.

In 1732 the country's first anglers' club, the Schuylkill
Fishing Club, was organized in Philadelphia, and around the
same time, maps of New York and New England, even military ones, often included twisting streaks marked "trout brook."
In their diaries, affluent colonials mentioned taking days off to
go fishing, but only some of these were fly fishers. George
Washington, though an avid fisherman, never took an interest
in artificial flies.

Many of the early fly fishers were English-born. Among
them was John Rowe, an affluent Boston merchant whose
claim to a place in history was that he owned some of the tea
that was dumped into Boston Harbor in 1773 from a place that
is now called Rowe's Wharf. Though remembered by some as

a revolutionary, Rowe was a smuggler and slave trader angered by British interference in trade. He had brought a two-piece fly rod with him from England and in his journal tells of trout fishing, sometimes with flies, in nearby rivers such as the Mashpee River on Cape Cod, where he claimed he caught several eighteen-inch trout. Those are large brook trout, but the Mashpee was and still is one of the few rivers from which some brook trout run to sea and return much larger than average size.

The New England Puritans spoke out against fly fishing. Why? Was it too much fun? Early twentieth-century journalist H. L. Mencken defined Puritanism as "the haunting fear that someone, somewhere, may be happy." Cotton Mather, one of the central religious leaders of New England Puritanism, was opposed to sports fishing of all kinds. He admitted to once having gone with friends "to divert ourselves at a famous fish pond," but only told this anecdote to explain that he fell in, nearly drowned, and rarely went fishing again. Among Puritans he was tremendously influential and when he wrote that when fishing, a net should be used, people listened. Fishing, like most activities of Puritan life, was to have a practical purpose, to achieve something, not to amuse. So fly fishing was unimaginable. Mather, who described rod fishing as "baiting and waiting, and how few taken," didn't get it.

In 1733 Joseph Seccombe, originally from an impoverished family in Medford, Massachusetts, but now a minister in Kingston, New Hampshire, delivered a sermon on fishing in which he distinguished between fishing for "business" and fishing for "diversion." Fishing for diversion was not acceptable. He stated, "He that takes pleasure in the Pains and dying agonies of any lower species of Creatures, is either a stupid sordid Soul, or a Murderer in Heart." The sermon was published anonymously and widely circulated.

Nonetheless, throughout the eighteenth century, the popularity of sports fishing in general and fly fishing in particular continued to grow. In 1762 the Mount Regale Fishing Company was founded and the lieutenant governor of Pennsylvania, Richard Penn, grandson of the founder of the colony, was a member. Other clubs started up at around the same time and some people were members of several clubs.

While on a trip to England, Richard Penn's daughter also became infatuated with fly fishing and acquired English rods. Most of the fly rods used during the pre-Revolutionary period were English-made—long, two-piece wooden rods—or American imitations. Even Benjamin Franklin, who encouraged people to buy American-made, used British fishing tackle. After the Revolution, though, as with many other products previously imported from Britain, American tackle started to dominate the market.

By the 1770s, fly fishing in America was no longer an English sport. Scattered records show that even before the Revolution, a few American rod-makers and fly-tiers had set up shop. In 1770 a Pennsylvania innkeeper, a Quaker named Davis Hugh Davis, sold flies that he had tied. This has led some to call him the first American fly-tier but there were, no doubt, others.

Tackle shops selling fly fishing equipment began to be established in port cities. In 1773 a Jeremiah Allen, about whom we know little, ran an ad for fly fishing tackle in the *Boston Newsletter*, and sometime in the 1770s, probably before the Revolution, a tackle shop opened on Market Street in Philadelphia. The store was owned by Edward Poole, who described himself as a "Fishing-Tackle-Maker." He started advertising in John Dunlap's *Pennsylvania Packet* in 1774 and offered a very broad range of tackle, including rods made of hazel, cedar, and dogwood, and an assortment of reels that were probably imported. He also sold a broad assortment of "artificial flies, moths and hackles," as he put it, and a variety of horsehair for lines.

Poole regularly claimed that he had the best-stocked tackle shop in Philadelphia, so there must have been several others, only one of which, William Ransted's, we know of. Poole also owned a tavern, the Wigwam, a fly fishers' lair by the Schuylkill, a favorite fly fishing river.

In 1788 Poole sold his business to George Lawton, who, judging by his ad, had an even larger selection of flies than Poole. Included in it were many non-insect fly fishing lures of the type still used today: minnows, mice, grasshoppers, and frogs. It is not known how long Lawton remained in business, but in 1803 he outfitted the Lewis and Clark expedition. The expedition did not purchase any fly fishing tackle from him, however.

In the early nineteenth century many Americans, including Washington Irving, regarded fly fishing as a peculiarly English activity, suitable for Britain's quiet rivers but not for the wilder American ones.

However, American sporting magazines with sections on fishing began to appear, indicating that fishing was becoming an important recreational activity in America. The first such magazine, published in 1829, was *American Turf Register and Sporting Magazine*. It mostly covered horse racing, but hunting and fishing were included. Most of its fly fishing articles were taken from British publications, as was the case with most other early American sporting magazines. In 1833 *The New-York and Annals of the American and English Turf* published a long essay on fly fishing that, according to historian Paul Schullery, was copied whole from an 1823 article in London's *Angler's Guide*.

Eventually, American fly fishing correspondents began to emerge. One early writer was George Gibson, who started fly fishing in Cumberland County, Pennsylvania, still a popular fly fishing destination today, in the 1790s. By the time he became a popular writer in the 1830s and 1840s, he was a very seasoned fly fisherman.

Gibson believed in using a wide variety of flies and in changing them regularly. There was a right fly for every pool, he said. He was the first American fly fishing guru, the predecessor of such twentieth-century writers as Roderick Haig-Brown, Lee Wulff, and Ray Bergman, who have produced an enormous body of fly fishing literature. Gibson and other early American fly fishing writers were very aware of what was being written in England, and either agreed or disagreed with it, but also presented their own theories based on their own fishing experiences.

During the decades before the Civil War, numerous other fly fishing writers, along with a growing number of fly fishers, emerged. Most popular among them was Frank Forester, a British-born American who also wrote romantic novels, which he considered his most important work, under his real name, Henry William Herbert. He regarded fly fishing writing as a lowly and embarrassing pursuit, but his fly fishing work was far more widely read than his novels. Many of his fly fishing articles were turned into popular books.

★ ★ ★

ALTHOUGH A NUMBER of out-of-state fly fishers had caught salmon in Maine as early as the 1830s, the people living there insisted for years that the Maine salmon would not take artificial flies. This was a recurring belief in the Americas, often encouraged by the British, who had the same outlook. That a salmon would bite at an artificial fly seemed so unlikely in the first place that many thought of the phenomenon as a curiosity of European rivers that didn't apply in wild America.

Then in 1885, a Bangor resident, Fred W. Ayer, caught six salmon in the Bangor Pool, a part of the Penobscot River where salmon gathered to prepare to leap over the Bangor Dam. Articles began to appear in sporting magazines about fly fishing

Fly fishing in Maine

for salmon on the Penobscot, and Maine salmon fly fishing came into fashion. Sadly, though, salmon largely vanished from the Penobscot within the next seventy years because 250 more dams were built along the river and industries were spewing waste into its waters.

Ironically, even as fly fishing was gaining in popularity in the United States after the Civil War, Atlantic salmon was vanishing from American rivers, not just in Maine, but throughout New England. New England had become an industrial center and dams were built on its principal rivers to power mills. Other rivers farther north were destroyed by the lumber and paper industries.

Starting in the late nineteenth century, the great adventure for the American fly fisher who could afford it was to fish for Atlantic salmon in Canada. This was their Norway. Wealthy Americans leased stretches of Canadian rivers and built fishing camps. There were numerous fabled salmon rivers in Labrador, Newfoundland, Quebec, and the Maritimes. Among them were the Restigouche (known in French as the Ristigouche), which flows 120 miles from the northern Appalachians in New Brunswick to Chaleur Bay in the Gulf of St. Lawrence in Quebec; and the Grand and Petit Cascapédia in Quebec. All are still considered among the world's greatest Atlantic salmon rivers.

In 1875 Genio C. Scott, in his encyclopedic *Fishing in American Waters*, wrote of fishing on the Canadian side of the border: "The fish are also much larger on this side. On an average, the scenery more majestic and the rivers more grand."

In the nineteenth century, it took a New Englander at least a month to get to a good Canadian salmon-fishing spot. The trip entailed taking a long train or boat ride, and then traveling

Fly fishing Atlantic salmon in the Grand Cascapédia, Quebec

a considerable distance by canoe. It was fly fishing for the few who had the time and money.

In October 1876 a lengthy article "Notes on Salmon Fishing" in *Scribner's Monthly* said that the Restigouche was still being fished mostly by Englishmen, as it had been since the time when the British soldiers were in Canada. The article recommended many other salmon-fishing rivers such as the Laval, the Godbout in Quebec, and the Moisie on the Labrador coast, and the Margaree in Cape Breton. The article also pointed out that some of Canada's best fishing was on Quebec's Gaspé Peninsula, but that the area was so remote it was "terra incognita, from which intelligence only came at intervals from small trading vessels or the long and tedious overland mail routes."

In Canada, the canoe earned a special place in fly fishing. Wrote Dean Sage in his 1888 classic *The Ristigouche and Its Salmon Fishing*, "The bark canoe is of all things that float the most graceful and picturesque. Local groups such as the Micmac fished salmon with a canoe and it became an indispensable part of Canadian fishing." The Native Americans considered their canoe-making skill a gift from the gods and believed that their handmade canoes were exact copies of the first canoe ever made.

While fishing from a boat is a step removed from standing in the life of a river, manipulating a canoe can make a fisher feel intensely part of its current. David James Duncan in *The River Why* describes a canoe as, "a silent water creature responsive to every surge and flex of current, gliding like a fingertip over a naked green body." On the great salmon rivers of Eastern Canada, traditional canoes made of bark are so delicate and require such careful handling that they are a deep, integral part of the fly fishing process.

Some fishers don't want to use a canoe because it involves developing a second body of knowledge as demanding as fly fishing itself. Stretches of rivers such as the Grand Cascapédia or the Bonaventure in Canada have sheer rock banks with thick forest rising above them, making them difficult to get to and hard to cast from, with few places in which to land a fish. Canada's rivers are often too deep and too fast for wading, and so big that they demand long rods. But long rods are awkward in canoes and so fishers are forced to use short ones and maneuver their canoes into the right position to catch the fish. The canoeist on the upstream side positions the vessel and the one on the downstream side fishes.

When a fish strikes, the fishers try to bring the canoe to a bank so that the downstream canoeist can play the fish and land it. But if the fish heads downstream, the fishers have no choice but to head after it.

IN THE SECOND half of the nineteenth century, while fly fishing was slowly catching on in Maine, it was also spreading throughout the continent. And the popularity of the sport was greatly helped along by the planting of trout in many rivers. In 1880 Fred Mather, a fishing writer and aquaculture enthusiast, arranged to ship eighty thousand German brown trout eggs from Germany to America aboard the *Werra*, a state-of-the-art German ocean liner that crossed the Atlantic in record-breaking time. Mather hatched the eggs at his Long Island Cold Spring Harbor hatchery and then took the fish to Pennsylvania, where the brown trout soon became well known. A heartier species than the rivers' native brook trout, they were then planted in rivers throughout the eastern United States and, eventually, the west. By the end of the century, most American trout rivers were home to both browns and rainbows.

Trout also began appearing in restaurants and cookbooks. Eliza Leslie's *Directions for Cookery*, the most popular American cookbook of the nineteenth century, published in sixty editions between 1837 and 1870, gave two recipes for trout, one boiled and one fried. Here is the fried version:

> Having cleaned the fish, and cut off the fins, dredge them with flour. Have ready some beaten yolk of egg, and in a separate dish some grated bread crumbs. Dip each fish into the egg, and then strew them with bread crumbs. Put some butter or fresh bee-dripping into a frying pan, hold

it over the fire till it is boiling hot; then (having skimmed it) put in the fish and fry them.

And here is the boiled one:

Put a handful of salt into the water. When it boils put in the trout. Boil them fast about twenty minutes, according to their size.

For sauce send with them melted butter, and put some soy into it, or flavor it with catchup. [This would probably be mushroom catsup, not tomato.]

A more sophisticated boiled trout comes from New York. After the Civil War, New Yorkers had become passionate about eating trout, and enormous quantities of fresh (or more or less fresh) trout started to be shipped to the city from Vermont and Maine. In 1869 Pierre Blot, a Frenchman who founded the New York Cooking Academy, wrote *Hand-Book of Practical Cookery, for Ladies and Professional Cooks*, in which he suggested serving trout with numerous sauces. Here is his good way to boil trout:

Clean and prepare about three pounds of fish, as directed for baking etc. It may be one fish or several according to size. Place the fish in a fish-kettle. Just cover it with cold water and a gill of vinegar, or with half water and half-wine: season with three or four sprigs of parsley, one of thyme. A bay leaf. One clove, one onion, half a carrot (in slices), two cloves of garlic, salt, pepper, and a little tarragon if handy. Set on the fire, and boil gently till done. Dish the fish, and serve it warm with a caper or anchovy sauce in a boat, or with currant jelly.

Of course, such recipes did not address the needs of fly fishers away on fishing trips wishing to cook their catch for dinner. The first rule when cooking a fish in the outdoors, expressed numerous times through the centuries, is to keep the fish intact. Do not cut it into steaks. A whole fish is a wonderfully sealed natural package. But if your fish is a large salmon, more than can be eaten at one meal, cut it into two fillets and save one.

Dean Sage advised splitting a fish down the back and grilling it, or, if you had more than twenty-four hours in camp, smoking it. Hemingway always cooked his trout in a frying pan with a lot of butter, salt, and pepper, and had a near-fetish of how a lemon must be squeezed onto a trout while it is frying, never added later. It surprises me that he was so citified that he would take butter with him when camping. Personally, the only thing I might add to my grilled fish is a pinch of salt. Don't let your salt be *fleur de sel*, though, or you will mark yourself as the wrong kind of fisher.

BY THE MID-NINETEENTH century, American fly fishing no longer belonged solely to the elite. John Brown, a leading fishing writer, reported the following in his publication *Angler's Almanac* in 1851:

> In the months of April and May the raftmen and lumbermen from the Delaware are seen in the fishing tackle of New York selecting, with the eyes of professors

of the art, the red, the black, and the gray hackle flies, which they use with astonishing effect on the wooded rivers of Pennsylvania.

But Brown was mostly referring to trout fishing. There was still tremendous skepticism among Americans about a salmon taking a fly. Little was understood about the salmon's life cycle or even about where they lived. John Brown authoritatively asserted that they could be found in the Mississippi River, which has never been true.

Until the mid-eighteenth century, it was not even understood that there were salmon in the Pacific or that they were a separate genus. In 1737 Georg Wilhelm Steller, a German naturalist from an impoverished background with few credentials in the scientific world, found Pacific salmon off Russia's Kamchatka Peninsula, one of a number of important natural discoveries he made while in the area. In 1741 Steller signed on to a Pacific expedition led by Vitus Jonassen Bering, a Danish mapmaker in the service of the Russians. Few survived that journey and Steller died of a fever. Impoverished locals dug his body up for the red cloak in which he was buried, and a pack of dogs finished off the corpse. The gravesite was washed away by the river in time. While in the Kamchatka, dropped off for a week of fishing in the wilderness with no means of communication or transportation, I often thought of Steller's ignominious end.

In the early 1790s in what is now British Columbia, British Navy explorer George Vancouver noticed thick schools of fish swarming by the mouths of rivers. Judging from the types of fishing tackle that his boat was carrying, he and his crew may have even tried to catch these fish, which must have been salmon.

In 1792 German naturalist Johann Julius Walbaum described the pacific salmon in a book titled *Artedi Piscium*. He used vernacular Russian to name five species of this genus, and these names have endured. Unfortunately, though, Walbaum did not realize that he had discovered a new genus and instead lumped his discoveries under *Salmo*, the genus of the Atlantic salmon that Europeans assumed included all salmon. It wasn't until 1866 that Albert Günther, a German zoologist at the British Museum, named the genus *Oncorhynchus*, derived from the Greek *onkos* meaning hook and *rynchos* meaning nose.

It is not known who first caught a Pacific salmon on a fly in the Americas. Frank Forester, the fly fishing writer who also wrote romantic novels, claimed that during the 1849 California gold rush, miners amused themselves in their spare time by fishing for salmon. And Haig-Brown tells a wonderful story that is probably an apocryphal "fish tale."

As Haig-Brown's story goes, the first to fly fish in British Columbia was Captain John Gordon, commander of the HMS *America*. He arrived at Fort Victoria at the time of the 1848 Oregon boundary dispute between the British and the Americans. The Hudson's Bay Company, the dominant commercial company in the Northwest, was represented in Victoria by Roderick Finlayson, who invited Gordon for breakfast one morning and served him local salmon. Upon seeing the fish, Gordon immediately became excited about the possibility of fly fishing. According to Finlayson, who recorded the event, "the Captain was preparing his fishing rod to fish for salmon with the fly, when I told him the salmon could not take the fly, but were fished here with bait." To a confirmed fly fisher like Gordon this was very disappointing news.

Finlayson provided Gordon with the appropriate tackle and bait and Gordon took a small boat and fished the mouth of the harbor. Hours later he returned with several good-size salmon, but all he said was, "What a country, where the salmon will not take the fly."

Up until this point the story is well documented and no doubt true. But now the disgruntled fly fisherman returned to London, and having been misinformed by a local, he told the commission trying to settle the territorial dispute to abandon the Oregon Territory because it was worthless—the salmon there would not take a fly. Given the amount of time it would have taken in the 1840s for a ship to travel from British Columbia, around the tip of South America, to London, it seems unlikely that Gordon got back before the negotiations were over. Of course, it also seems unlikely that the British would give up the Oregon Territory because the salmon there did not take a fly. But give up the Oregon Territory they did, and it is significant that a substantial number of people, probably all fly fishers, believed this story.

While fly fishing had started to catch on along the West Coast, tackle shops had not. The western fishers had not yet learned to build rods or even tie flies. An article in an 1857 sporting magazine claimed that westerners were forced to be bait fishers because there were no tackle shops. But this was not quite true. There was fly fishing in the West for trout, salmon, and steelhead going back to the mid-nineteenth century. Written accounts, often by British visitors, testify to this. Some described catching huge, hard-fighting salmon, probably king. Flies were either brought from England or tied.

Government agents throughout the West in the mid-nineteenth century started seeing locals fly fishing. In the

1860s, at the height of the Sioux Wars, a government naturalist saw soldiers taking large trout with artificial flies at the headwaters of the Missouri. This agent wrote of officers and men crowding the river banks, catching so many fish that they could feed their entire command. He called the fish "Lewis Trout" after Meriwether Lewis of the Lewis and Clark expedition. Judging from the Lewis's and Clark's journals, Lewis does not appear to have been a great fisherman, but Silas Goodrich, a skilled fly fisher, was with the expedition and provided much food. Lewis, writing about Goodrich's catch in his journal, was the first to describe the cutthroat trout.

According to a 1904 book by A. C. Laut, *Pathfinders of the West*, the fabled and ill-fated Seventh Calvary, had its share of fly fishermen. Captain Frederick Benteen and his men seldom passed up a good fly fishing opportunity, of which there were many in the virgin rivers of Montana. According to his troops, the captain frequently dismounted and waded into a river to catch a few trout.

Benteen was openly critical of his commander, General George Armstrong Custer, whom he thought vain, self-aggrandizing, and reckless with the lives of his men. Tired of criticism from this insubordinate officer, Custer sent him and his H Company off on an insignificant side action, while he and his men rode off to "glory," fighting against Sitting Bull and his warriors.

Meanwhile, the Commanding General Alfred Terry sent out another column of cavalry under the command of General George Crook. Crook blundered into the Battle of Rosebud near the Yellowstone River, where he was badly defeated in June 1876 by Crazy Horse. While Crazy Horse went on to the Little Big Horn, Crook retreated to Goose Creek, where he and his men had previously enjoyed excellent trout fishing. Badly bruised from battle, they took a week off to do more fly fishing by the creek with artificial flies and grasshoppers, reportedly landing at least five hundred trout.

As for Benteen, a year later, on September 13, 1877, he led a charge of his company against the retreating Nez Perce, carrying and waving a fly rod as he urged his men on. After the tribe's defeat, the final defeat of the Indian Wars, the Nez Perce's Chief Joseph asked to meet the crazy officer who had charged with a fishing rod. It was arranged, but we do not know what they spoke about. Trout?

Historians like to say that Benteen was the last American soldier to go into battle with a fly rod. Apparently, they don't know about Jack Hemingway, the man who parachuted behind German lines with a fishing rod during World War Two.

FOR DECADES, WESTERN fly fishers used East Coast flies or sometimes British flies. It was not until the end of the century that local western fly patterns started to be developed.

Even in the West, where people celebrated living in the wild and verdant nature, fly fishing was not originally pursued by people who lived near the great rivers. Rather, as in the East, it was the passion of city people wanting a trip into the countryside. Fly fishing and conservation movements became united: both fought to save fish by making them the exclusive domain of sports fishers. The anglers and conservationists had a certain amount of political clout because it was becoming apparent that there was more income to be had from fly fishing tourism than from commercial fishing. Fly fishing drew affluent people eager to spend money. In 1925, at the urging of fly fishers, Washington

State banned the sale of steelhead, and in 1928 Oregon severely restricted commercial steelhead fisheries.

This movement angered Native Americans. Commercial steelhead fishing was a traditional way of life for them.

In 1935 Oregon fly fishers tried to get steelhead declared a trout to make it ineligible for commercial fishing. The commercial fishing of trout, considered a game fish, had already been gradually banned everywhere in the United States. With the backing of a delegation from the Northern Willamette Valley, an area known for its fly fishing, the measure passed the State House but was turned down in the Senate after ichthyologists assured the legislators that a steelhead, though descended from a rainbow trout, was a salmon.

Steelhead remained commercial fish in Oregon until 1975, and other species of Pacific salmon have remained both commercial and sports fish throughout the West Coast states. The commercial fishing of Atlantic salmon has been greatly reduced, and today in both Canada and Europe salmon is primarily a sports fish.

While the profits from commercial fishing have been declining, profits from sports fishing have been steadily rising. This is particularly true of fly fishing because it draws an affluent crowd. There are now more than 3.8 million fly fishers in the United States and that number is steadily growing. Much of the economic boom can be seen in the increased number of fishing lodges, fishing guides, tackle shops, and other services for visiting fishers.

State fish and game agencies are also part of this fishing economy. The first state agency was established in Massachusetts in 1865, and one by one, every other state also established its own agency, primarily to work on wildlife conservation. These agencies receive little or no funding from the government. Most of their operating budget comes from the sale of hunting and fishing licenses. This has meant, for better and for worse, that the agencies actively work to encourage hunting and fishing, and are especially interested in bringing in out-of-state hunters and fishers.

As the agencies gained traction, licenses started to be required by law, at a low rate for locals and a higher one for visitors. The first fishing license in Oregon, in 1909, cost one dollar for residents and five dollars for out-of-staters. The state agencies worked in partnership with sports fishers to promote sports fishing and discourage commercial fishing. Fly fishing was promoted everywhere from New York to Alaska with the help of state fish and game agencies.

Even as fly fishing was expanding in America, it was also becoming a far more international sport. Fly fishing for salmon and trout is now an important tourist attraction of Australia, New Zealand, and Chile.

Argentina started its fly fishing tourism industry in the early twentieth century with the help of mostly British guides. Fly fishing in Tierrra del Fuego, an archipelago at the southern tip of South America, took hold and it has become a major fly fishing destination. The more rugged and remote a region, the greater it seems to appeal to fly fishers. There are now fishing trips to Greenland and to both the Kamchatka Peninsula and the Kola Peninsula in Russia. Lodges and transportation provided by unwieldy beat-up Soviet helicopters cater to fishers willing to pay thousands of dollars for exotic fishing experiences. Or, at an equal or even greater expense, anglers can choose to fish for the endangered taimen in Mongolia.

The Southern Hemisphere offers summer fishing during the Northern Hemisphere's winter when there is little fly fishing in America or Europe. So, if you have enough money, you can now fly fish year-round.

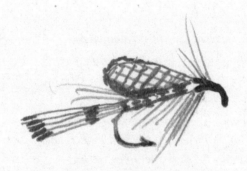

Queen of the waters fly

6

It's About the Fly

When if an insect falls (his certain guide)
He gently takes him from one whirling tide;
Examines well his form with anxious eyes,
His gaudy colours, wings, horns, and size.
Then round his hook a proper fur he winds,
    And in the back a speckled feather binds
    So just the properties in ev'ry part,
That even nature's hand revive in art.

—JOHN GAY, *RURAL SPORTS*, 1713

I once asked a retired New York City Ballet dancer why little girls wanted to be ballerinas. She said, "It's about the tutu." In a similar way, fly fishing is about the fly. The fly is whimsical, imaginative, with the suggestion of magic. It gives beauty and grace. The artificial fly is the tutu of fishing.

There are thousands of flies in endless shapes and sizes, made from a long list of materials of different textures and colors. Even if you don't fish, you could spend an enjoyable hour in a good tackle shop inspecting flies. If the choice had remained limited to just a few dingy furry things, like the twelve flies of the fifteenth-century *Treatyse*, fly fishing might not have caught on as it did, though fishers may have caught the same amount of fish. Because the flies are so beautiful and so mysterious and there are thousands of them, they are even more irresistible to humans than they are to fish. There have been some great fly-tiers, who never went fishing. They just liked flies.

Some fishers will fish all day, or even all week, with the same reliable fly. Others will change their fly every third cast. I am somewhere in between. I believe that a fish's interests are limited. If I am fishing with a light-colored fly and take no fish, I might switch to a darker color, but I don't make frequent switches.

Part of the attraction, the lore, and, forgive me, the lure of flies is the fanciful names they are given, names such as "queen of the waters," "rat-face MacDougall," "crazy Charlie," "anni-hilator," "fiery dragon," "royal coachman," and, when someone finally ran short on inspiration, the "no name."

Haig-Brown thought there were thirty thousand different "recognized" flies, while pointing out that there were also many other "unrecognized" ones. Sometimes a fisher who regularly fishes a certain hole will invent a fly for that spot, and if it is not a famous hole, few other anglers will ever know about this fly.

Nobody knows why a fish takes a certain fly and not another. Sometimes in clear water you can see a trout bring his nose up close to a fly and then decide against it and swim off. Fish, like cats and unlike dogs, are careful about what they eat. They seem to know that the wrong fly can be dangerous. Many hooked fish escape and perhaps they learn. Experience makes them more cautious. Once a fly has grabbed a fish by the lip and yanked it through the water, the fish never looks at insects quite the same way again.

For the angler, this is the great advantage of a river that has not been fished a great deal. The fish in a wilderness river like the Ozernaya in the northern Kamchatka seem naïve, though if the Russians find enough affluent foreigners to helicopter in, this may one day change.

No one can say for certain, though many try, what a fish wants or why it chooses the fly it does. And that is the fun of the whole thing. I always feel as if I am trying to talk a fish into something. I am the crooked salesman offering bad merchandise. If they take what I cast, they will be sorry.

Ozernaya River, Kamchatka, Russia

Anyone who watches a fish in a stream will see that it considers all sorts of things to eat, including perhaps a leaf, which it will then spit out. If it chooses something more exotic, with a sharp hook, it may try to spit it out, too, and often succeeds, which is why fishers do what is known as "setting the hook." Sometimes, especially with trout, this means no more than giving the rod a hard yank, though if you do this too soon, you will remove the fly from the fish's mouth. When setting the hook with a salmon, it is advisable to slowly pull the line to one side while hoping that you are pulling in the right direction, into the fish and not away from it.

With salmon, especially Atlantic, it is advisable to wait a few seconds before setting the hook. A fisher in Galway, Ireland, told me to say "God save the Queen," before pulling. This is British advice and when I repeated it to a fisher in Cork, she said that she couldn't believe that any Irish fisher would say such a thing.

In truth, most ideas on which flies to use and how to handle them are not based on science. It is mostly just a question of personal experience. Guides and authors offering advice are very experienced fishers who have arrived at their beliefs after many years of catching, and failing to catch, fish.

Increasingly, though, fishers are turning to science. They are studying the mineral content of the water and its oxygen level. Studies have been conducted on which species prefer which colors. Some species, it has been found, are drawn to ultraviolet light, and so some fishers now fish with an ultraviolet-light pen that they can pass over their fly box to choose an ultraviolet fly. The fear is that through science, we will uncover all there is to be known about fish and fly fishing will lose its mystery. Debate will end. But that is not likely. Science always raises as many questions as it answers.

Adams fly

There are two kinds of flies: imitators and attractors. Imitators are fake flies made to get the fish to mistake them for the real ones that are also floating in the water. Attractors are flies that look "buggy" but do not resemble any known insect. An Adams, one of the most popular flies, looks like an insect, but no known insect looks like an Adams. And some fishers succeed in catching fish with a purple Adams, which definitely does not resemble any natural insect. The Adams I tie is fluffier than most, due to my lack of tying skill, but I don't think the fish mind.

An Adams has a tail. Such tails are usually not characteristic of insects, but they create movement in the water, which attracts fish. The artificial fly literally wags its tail at the fish. Also, a tail can hide a hook's point, which tends to be exposed since most of the fly is tied on a hook's shank.

Some salmon and steelhead flies have hooks that are attached to their tails rather than their bodies. One such salmon fly is the large and feathery Dalai Lama. I assume this name is an intentional sacrilege, because Tibetan Buddhists, including their leader, the Dalai Lama, believe that it is wrong to fish. But maybe I am mistaken, maybe no irony was intended. The flies are also often called Dolly Lamas. I have caught both sockeye and chum salmon and even large rainbow on these odd contraptions that resemble nothing in nature but have a wiggly hook.

Haig-Brown called into question the whole idea of imitation flies by pointing out that although there are thirty thousand or more recognized flies, a trout probably eats only about one thousand kinds of insects. And even though it is an insectivore, a trout also eats many other things, such as shrimp, crabs, frogs, and mice, which, like some insects, fall into the river from the bank. Fly-tiers imitate these things also.

Bomber fly

There is a fly called a bomber, made from bunching together squirrel tail fur and deer hair, that is designed to look like a cigar butt. Fishers do not smoke cigars as much as they used to, although the smoke drives away mosquitoes and the lit end is good for trimming line, but in the days when they did smoke them, salmon would often swallow the discarded cigar butts, and so this fly was invented. Bombers can work, and are often just casually tossed in the water so that they land like discarded butts. This crude style of landing inspired their name.

Some flies are called streamers. Usually tied on long-shanked hooks, they are large flies that are moved through the water in imitation of small fish. Some are named minnows but there is a certain politesse to calling small fish imitations minnows. In truth what the trout are often eating that makes them chase these "minnows" is not minnows but very young trout or salmon.

Artificial flies are certainly more realistic than the wooden, metal, or plastic artificial lures used in other types of fishing. A bass will take a fly, especially a minnow fly, but a salmon will never take a bass plug. Zane Grey argued that a bass plug was an insult to the fish's intelligence. It offended him. He believed in treating salmonids with more respect.

Some fishers buy their flies and there is a logic to this. Flies that are for sale are usually of excellent quality, and shop owners can steer you toward those flies that are being successfully used in local waters at the time of your visit. A small dry fly, like an Adams, is tiny and delicate and difficult to tie for many fishers, but well-tied ones can be found in any fly fishing shop.

Haig-Brown suggested fishing with no more than six fly patterns, though many anglers, including myself, have had success with fewer than this. Lee Wulff believed that salmon find many salmon flies indistinguishable from each other. A fish only sees a fly from below looking up, and so can't appreciate its full beauty and complexity. If we humans judged flies from a fish's viewpoint, we would create much simpler confections, but what would be the fun in that?

In his 1960s cult classic, *Trout Fishing in America*, Richard Brautigan, one of America's great absurdists, perfectly satirizes the importance that fishers attach to flies. Brautigan writes that Leonardo da Vinci came to him in a dream. The artist was working in a tackle shop, laboring until he had made the ultimate fly, which he called "the Last Supper." When his employers saw it, they fainted, and word of the fly soon spread. Writes Brautigan, "In a matter of months that trout fishing lure was the sensation of the twentieth century, far outstripping such shallow accomplishments as Hiroshima or Mahatma Gandhi. Millions of the Last Supper were sold in America. The Vatican ordered ten thousand and they didn't even have any trout there. Testimonials poured in. Thirty-four ex-presidents of the United States all said, 'I caught my limit on "The Last Supper".'"

★ ★ ★

FLY FISHING TENDS to attract obsessive personalities. The worst are the fly-tiers.

In earlier times fishers tied their own flies. They also forged their own hooks, built their own rods, and braided their own lines. Fly fishing was a different pursuit back then when all this manufacturing skill was required. Today, you can buy everything you need and concentrate on the fishing itself. Most any kind of fly can be purchased. They are not even expensive.

So why tie flies? Almost no one makes their own hooks, or lines anymore and only a few make rods. The standard excuse is that tying flies gives you something to do in the off-season. The idea that you have to find a way to remain involved in fly fishing in the winter is in itself obsessive. The truth is that people enjoy tying flies. How else to explain the fact that there are many skilled tiers in famous fly fishing areas who don't even fish?

Sometimes local tackle stores buy flies from colorful local characters. Jerry Doak, a New Brunswick fly-tier whose father owned a tackle shop, was fascinated by local tiers. When interviewed by writer Judith Dunham, he reminisced about Burt Miner, an old-time tier who made copper killers, a feathery red brown and black salmon fly. "He was a heavy smoker who rolled his own cigarettes. There was so much smoke in the room that I could barely see the fly in the vise. He would roll a cigarette with one hand and tie a copper killer with the other." While many of the best local flies are tied by such local characters, the standard flies, sold inexpensively in tackle shops were often tied by Asian women who had been given the pattern and will never in their lives fish. But many of the famous tiers also never fished. They just like to tie flies.

Baseball great Ted Williams, who regularly demonstrated his phenomenal hand–eye coordination in Fenway Park, was a fly fisherman, and probably a great one. Babe Ruth was also a fly fisherman of undoubtedly considerable skill. Williams enjoyed tying his own flies. He said he did it to unwind after a game. "It relaxes me," he explained. "I used to tie flies during the season, come in after a game all taut and nervous, tie a few flies and, boom, right to sleep."

People like flies. Many are hung as decoration and never fished. Famous fly-tiers understand this. English tier Stewart Canham said, "A large portion of the flies I tie end up being framed. I don't mind. The important part is that I enjoy tying the fly."

Like all addictions, the fly-tying obsession comes on slowly. First you tie one fly for the experience. Then you tie another to do a better job. Then you think, maybe this fly would look better with a red head. Or maybe a small strip of flashy metallic something. Soon you have filled a box.

One of the great contemporary fly-tiers, Poul Jorgensen, compared fly-tying to his experience of learning to play musical scales as a child. You start out simply and then get better and better.

Fly-tying is good for writers because writers are always looking for distractions to take them away from their desk. After writing for a while, you can hop over to that table and tie a quick woolly bugger, a simple variation on the nineteenth-century woolly worm, and then go back to work. Or, if you want a longer diversion, you can tie a more complicated and creative salmon fly. With salmon flies, you feel free to do almost anything. You could buy any of these flies, of course, but if you tie your own, you will be ready with them when the season

opens. Some say that fishing with your own flies is more satisfying than using store-bought ones; it is more fun to know that
you personally have deceived the fish. When you tie your own
fly, even of a classic pattern, you get to test your own theories
of what a fly should be.

Tying flies is not exactly about tying. It does not require
nimble fingers executing complicated knots. Most flies have
no knots at all. Tying is mostly about fastening objects to the
shaft of a hook by wrapping thread around them. For the obsessive personality, that wrapping process itself can be very
satisfying.

MOST EARLY ACCOUNTS of fly fishing, even the ancients,
describe flies, so we know that they have had a slow evolution.
Even ancient Roman flies, if tied light and well enough, might
still catch fish today, and some of the flies recommended in
the fifteenth-century *Treatyse* are still, with some variation,
in use.

From ancient times to the Elizabethan era, flies were generally made with wool bodies. That was a mistake, and one that
many fly fishers still make. Humans tend to judge a fly when
it is dry, whereas the fish sees it when it is wet. Wet wool and
dry wool look very different from one another.

All the twelve flies of the *Treatyse* have wool bodies. They
are sorted by the months of the year. Here are the flies recommended for the month of May:

> The Yellow Fly: the body of yellow wool, the wings of
> the red cocks hackle and the drake dyed yellow. The Black
> Leaper: the body of black wool and lapped about with

the herl of the peacocks tail; and the wings of a red capon
with a blue head.

The Haslinger Breviary from Austria, in the same century as
the *Treatyse*, offers twenty-one fly patterns, all also arranged by
month. There is a logic to this that a modern fly fisher under-
stands. I use completely different flies in the Big Wood in
October than I do in March because different aquatic insects
are hatching. The midges of March are gone by October.

The Austrian fishing season runs from May to November.
For some months, the *Breviary* even recommends changing fly
patterns. For some months, it even recommends changing
fly patterns in the middle of the same month, but mysteri-
ously, it suggests no fly patterns for the month of July. The book
also advises tying flies on different-size hooks and using larger-
size hooks for less-than-clear water, a choice with which many
modern fishers would agree.

The *Breviary*'s flies are trout flies, though they possibly might
also have been used for grayling. The feathers described are
only identified by their color, but given Austria's geography,
they probably came from partridge, heron, and both green and
white woodpeckers.

The *Breviary* was the first book to depart from recom-
mending tying flies with wool. It advised using wrapped silk
thread of yellow, red, brown, blue, gold, silver, gray, or black
instead. These flies had the advantage of being lighter and less
apt to become waterlogged than wool flies. Austria had no silk
industry, but nearby northern Italy did and may have been the
source of the thread.

Other early books that recommended using silk to tie flies
were the hand-written codex from the Bavarian monastery in

Tegernsee, which included fifteen flies, and *The Little Treatise on Fishing* by the Spaniard Fernando Basurto. Neither book offered detailed instructions, just information on the color of the feathers and silk thread to be used.

By the seventeenth century, Walton's contemporaries were offering sound fly-tying advice that is still of value today. Robert Venables said that determining whether to use a fly that sinks or one that floats requires daily study of how the fish are feeding, and he invented a way of weighting the hook so that the fly rested slightly deeper in the water. He also said that the fisher had to examine the insect life along the bank to determine what kind of fly to use and to pay particular attention to the insect's belly, since that was what the trout saw.

Venables was an innovative fly-tier. Sometimes he would tie a fly with the hook pointing up instead of down and the feathery wings pointing toward the head instead of the tail—an upside-down fly. It is not clear why he did this or whether it worked. Not many fishers do the same today, though there are some upside-down flies such as the Crazy Charlie or the Clouser minnow. Venables also suggested that fly fishing would work not only for salmonids, but also for roach, bream, pike, and other fish.

Walton had so little to say about flies that it is wondered how much he used them. He did say of angling, "Is it not an art to deceive a fish with an artificial fly?" But he was certainly no fly-tier. He wrote, "I confess, no direction can be given to make a man of dull capacity able to make a fly well." The little there is on flies in his book was lifted from *The Art of Angling*, published in 1651 by his friend Thomas Barker. A true fish expert, Barker gives directions for tying a dozen fly patterns, mostly trout-fly patterns, but also one for salmon. It is significant that he gives a salmon-fly pattern because fishing historians often credit James Chetham's 1681 book, *The Angler's Vade Mecum*, published thirty years later, as the first to mention flies made specifically for salmon.

What is exceptional about Barker is that he was the first to give detailed directions on how to tie flies. In one pattern, he uses a technique called palmering, still employed today, which involves bending a feather backward so that its hairs stick out, creating what are known as hackles. A number of Barker's flies, such as the mayfly, are still in common use.

Here are his instructions for the Palmer fly:

> We will begin to make the Palmer-flye. You must arm your line on the in-side your hook, then take your sizzers and cut so much of the browne of the Mallards feather as in your owne reason shall make the wings, then lay the outermost part of the feather near the hook, and the point of the feather next toward the shank of the hook, so whip it three or four times about the hook with the same silk you armed the hook with, so make your silk fast; then you must take the hackle of a cock or capon, or a plovers top feather, then take the hackle, silk, or cruell, gold or silver thred, make all fast at the bent of the hook, then begin to work with the cruell [a twisted smooth and flattened wool yarn], and silver thred, work it up to the wings, every bout shifting your fingers and making a stop, then the cruell and silver will fall right, then make fast, then work up the hackle to the same place, then make the hackle fast; then you must take the hook betwixt your fingers and thumb in the left hand, with a needle or pin part the wings in two, so take the silk you have wrought

with all this while, and whip once about the shank that falleth crosse betwixt the wings; than with your thumb you must turn the point of the feather towards the bent of the hook, so view the proportion.

Barker was also the first to write about, if not the inventor of, "dubbing." This technique involves placing a gnarl of animal hair around a thread that is wrapped around the shank of a hook to create the body of the fly. Barker wrote, "If you make the grounds of Hogs wooll, sandy black or white, or the wooll of a Bear, or of a two year old red Bullock, you must work all the grounds upon a waxed silk." When dubbing, you can still make the fly's body out of wool or fur, but it is more lightweight for casting and doesn't become as dark and sodden as other wool bodies because light passes through it, giving it a translucent glow. Dubbing is a technique still commonly used today, usually with synthetic materials. An Adams is an example of a modern fly that uses dubbing to make the body.

Charles Cotton, the young poet and fisherman friend of Walton, was one of the great pioneer fly-tiers. In the twelve chapters that he added to Walton's book, he gives directions for tying more than sixty flies, all imitations of real insects. He did not believe in attractor flies. Given the limited area in which he fished, it is extraordinary that he found sixty different aquatic insects to imitate. However, some of his flies do not resemble any insect that can be identified.

Cotton appears to have been an early entomologist, well versed in the habits and life cycles of the insects that he was re-creating. He did not claim to have invented any of the flies he wrote about, and so his list is thought to be a collection of flies commonly used in seventeenth-century Britain. Cotton did not use much exotic material, but he was extremely resourceful in finding local materials, including dog, bear, hog ear, martin, cow, aborted calf, and even, from somewhere, camel fur. He used these materials when dubbing, a technique that he describes in much greater detail than Barker. He suggests that after a fly is finished, a needle be used to make the dubbing hairs stick out, a technique that is still used today.

FLY-TYING, A FAIRLY stable craft for centuries, began to undergo changes in the 1800s. Far more books were being published then than in previous centuries, and that included books on fly fishing. New ideas, and with them new flies, were being presented.

William C. Stewart's 1857 *The Practical Angler: or, The Art of Trout-fishing, more particularly applied to clear water*, had a tremendous influence on fishing and fly-tying. In his book, Stewart promoted (but did not invent) the concept of casting upstream. With this type of cast, the fly is caught in a strong downstream drift, and so appears to have a great deal of natural movement. Flies with tails and longer wings and hackles began to be developed to accommodate upstream casting.

It is not certain how much influence Stewart had on Thaddeus Norris, often called "the father of American fly fishing," but Norris also championed upstream casting. He promoted the idea that American rivers and fish were different from English rivers and fish. His 1864 *The American Angler's Book* defined American fly fishing and presented new ideas on casting and tackle, including fly-tying. Before Norris, Americans fished with British flies. Now, they started tying and fishing with distinctly American flies. These new American flies were

Flies for April, Pl. VII., *The Fly-Fisher's Entomology*, Ronalds, Longman, Brown, Green, and Longmans, London, 1856

No. 10: Golden Dun Midge. Order: Diptera. Family: Tripulidae. Genus: *Chironomus*. Species: *plumosus*

No. 11: Sand Fly. Order: Trichoptera. Family: Phryganidae. Genus: *Limnephilus*. Species: *flavus*

No. 12: Stone Fly. Order: Neuroptera. Family: Perlidae. Genus: *Perla*. Species: *bicaudata*

Stewart's black spider fly

more imaginative than the British flies and often did not strictly imitate real insects.

Another huge nineteenth-century change was that as transportation improved, fishing for salmon became much more popular. It also became more feasible, as better lines and rods had been developed. This opened up a debate that has remained unresolved. Why do salmon take flies and what kind of flies appeal to them?

For centuries, many scientists and curious anglers have cut open the stomachs of salmon that return to their rivers after their sojourns to the sea. Without exception, they have found their stomachs empty. Once a salmon returns to a river, it no longer eats. This is part of the natural design. When a salmon goes to sea, it spends years growing to many times the size of the smolt it was when it first left the river. It gains 95 percent of its full size while at sea and accomplishes this by being a voracious predator, gobbling everything it can find—shrimp, crabs, smaller fish, zooplankton. Such an animal would be a disaster in a river. It would eat most every creature, including all the fish, which would kill off the trout and even new generations of young salmon. Mammals and bird predators would starve. A school of such salmon could clean out a river in a matter of weeks.

But this doesn't happen, because once salmon return to their rivers, they stop eating. Thanks to their rich ocean diet, they have built up enough fat and protein, and stored enough energy, to make the arduous journey upriver against the current, leaping waterfalls, shooting rapids, getting back to their place of birth to spawn. After spawning, they have spent all they have and they die. The exception is a few Atlantic salmon that survive spawning to go back to sea and return to spawn again. They are known as kelts. But there are very few kelts. Except for steelhead, Pacific salmon rarely return as kelts.

So if the salmon are not eating real flies, why do they every now and then swallow an artificial fly? There are almost as many theories about this as there are salmon fly fishers. Some say it is because the salmon have memories of when they were juveniles in the river feeding on flies. But if that were true, why is it that they never swallow a live insect? Some say that if a fly is large, colorful, and outlandish enough, the salmon will find it irritating and so snap at it. Others say that such a fly whets a salmon's curiosity. And still others say that a good fly-tier can make an artificial fly irresistible—more irresistible than anything found in nature. Lee Wulff compared the salmon's urge to bite an artificial fly to the urge of a boy to cross the street just to kick a can. My guide on the River Blackwater in Ireland, a slightly plumpish woman named Glenda Powell who is always dieting, said, "I'm not supposed to eat chocolate but every once in a while someone will pass a chocolate in front of me and I'll just grab it."

Megan Boyd, Scotland's great salmon fly-tier of the twentieth century, said, "You can say what you want but everyone is puzzled over why a salmon takes a fly."

Whatever the reason, most fishers agree that a salmon fly should look nothing like a real insect but should be flashy and noticeable. Starting in the eighteenth century, it was also believed that salmon flies need to be large. Barker wrote that salmon flies should be tied to large hooks with six wings, as opposed to the usual two. Richard Bowlker in the mid-eighteenth century wrote, "Salmon will take almost any of the flies used for trout, if made larger than usual." This idea that salmon flies need to be large endured into the twentieth century, but its logic—that a large fish wants something large to bite on—is faulty. It has since been clearly demonstrated that even the largest salmon will bite on a small fly.

Another eighteenth-century notion has proven to be more enduring. Bowlker wrote that salmon flies should be "gaudy," and throughout the eighteenth century and even more so in the nineteenth, salmon flies became ever more ostentatious. The Irish were the first to tie large and gaudy salmon flies, but the English and Scots soon followed. Today's flies are somewhat less flashy than their predecessors, but still very colorful.

Because salmon flies were more extravagant, more creative, than other flies, there was an urge to showcase them in books, and in this way certain flies became well known and frequently copied. George Bainbridge published the first book with color illustrations of salmon flies, called *The Fly Fisher's Guide*, in 1816. In it, he presented five salmon flies in hand-colored engravings. By the standards of later in the century, they were very modest flies, made with bodies of dyed wool and wings from turkeys that had probably been raised specifically for supplying feathers to fly-tiers.

By 1842, when William Blacker's *Art of Fly Making* was published, salmon flies had changed considerably. Blacker was not raising chickens and turkeys for his flies. He was using cock-of-the-rock and macaw feathers from South America, blue kingfisher feathers from India, and the crests of iridescent Himalayan monal pheasants.

Blacker gave detailed tying instructions and suggested which British rivers were suitable for each of his flies. But he cautioned

Atlantic salmon leaping a waterfall in the Scottish Highlands

that the colors of the flies had to be exactly right. It was not good enough to use blue, it had to be Prussian blue, or cinnamon brown, or sooty olive. At this point, if you have a suspicious nature, you may have guessed what Blacker was up to. He was not only selling his books and flies, but was also in the business of selling exotic feathers. In Blacker's day, rare birds, most living in far-flung corners of the world, were not protected.

For those who could not afford the feathers of exotic birds, Blacker did give recipes for dyeing ordinary feathers exotic colors—turmeric, ground alum, and tartar crystals could turn an ordinary feather parrot yellow. But Blacker understood that such were down-market solutions, and fly fishers were generally an up-market crowd. They wanted the best and were

King Fisher Fly from the J. R. Harris Collection, 1791

willing to pay for it. He gave a list of thirty-seven birds whose plumage should be owned by any serious fly fisher. Not by coincidence, most of these birds, such as the resplendent quetzal and the bird of paradise, are now considered endangered.

The resplendent quetzal, which resides in the remote Central American highlands and is only rarely seen today, was a favorite of fly-tiers. A friendly looking round-headed bird, it has feathers of a brilliant, almost iridescent green. The male's two tail feathers are nearly three feet long and undulate in flight. The quetzal is the origin of a deity, the winged serpent, found in most early Meso-American cultures.

The bird of paradise, when it is found at all, is found mostly in Indonesia and Papua New Guinea. Westerners have been hunting this bird since at least 1522, when Magellan's crew gave some to the king of Spain. The Spanish often took off the skin for the feathers and when they did, they cut off the feet. So what westerners saw of these birds had spectacular feathers and no feet. This led many westerners to believe that a bird of paradise had no feet and spent its life in midair, even laying its eggs on the backs of other birds in flight, all of which made it seem like an even more exotic creature. Europeans understood nothing about these birds until naturalists began studying them in the mid-nineteenth century, but popes and kings posed with them, and Rembrandt, Bruegel, and Rubens painted them.

The male bird of paradise sprouts spectacular long fluffy feathers when mating, but the birds have been hunted for so long that nature, through evolution, has provided them with a protective device. Some males will mate before they begin sprouting, thereby protecting the continuance of their species, though not entirely protecting them, and they remain in considerable danger today.

The worldwide growth of fly-tying in the nineteenth century was just one small part of a much larger cultural phenomenon, the expansion of the British Empire. At the time, the empire was a source of great British pride—the idea that they owned most of the world. A manifestation of this pride was the taking of souvenirs. Every British subject could own little pieces of Britain's many global possessions. Collecting became very popular, and many affluent English living rooms had cases filled with stones, beetles, butterflies, and feathers from all over the world.

Nineteenth-century ships of conquest exploring the empire routinely took a scientist or naturalist with them.

Some had great scientific minds. Charles Darwin was one. Others were influential men from royal societies out to identify and name as many species as possible after themselves. Some were ignored by the officers running the voyage such as poor George Steller in the Kamchatka. But some of these men returned with troves of specimens and sometimes built great reputations for themselves. Institutions were also involved. Among those feverishly acquiring feathers was the British Museum.

One of the by-products of all this was a craze for feathers, which spread from England to Europe and America. Feathers on women's hats became a passion among affluent women. Sometimes a hat would display an entire feather-covered bird skin and be so large that its wearer would struggle to fit in a carriage.

In the Paris market, feathers were sold in bulk. A hunter would kill eight hundred or more birds to sell a kilo of feathers. In 1775 Marie Antoinette, while she still had a head, appeared with an egret plume decorated with diamonds woven into her high and complicated hairstyle. At the time, there were already twenty-five feather fashion shops, known as *plumassiers*, in France. A century later there were almost three hundred.

According to one book on the feather craze, *Feather Fashions and Bird Preservation* by Robin W. Doughty, in 1886 a concerned ornithologist walked through a fashionable New York shopping district and counted seven hundred hats with bird feathers and three quarters of them displayed entire bird skins. That was the look: it appeared as though an exotic bird was perched on a woman's head.

By the end of the nineteenth century, millions of pounds of feathers were being imported to France, England, and

America. That means that an enormous number of birds were being killed. In the United States alone, an estimated two hundred million North Americans birds were killed every year for their plumage—and theirs were not even the most sought-after feathers.

By the end of the century the most desired feathers were becoming scarce, which only meant that the prices became extremely high and therefore they were great status symbols.

Fly-tiers were by no means immune to the feather craze. A trout fisher making a mayfly or caddis had no need for exotic feathers, but those making salmon flies came up with the wildest concoctions imaginable. This despite the fact that no one knew what a salmon might like.

One of the most influential of these new salmon flies was invented by a gillie. *Ghillie*, or more correctly, *ghillie dhu*, is a Gaelic word originally referring to a guardian spirit of trees. In stories, he is a kind but wild creature, shy and dressed in leaves and moss, but in the real world, especially in Britain, he is a working-class local dressed in a tweed sports coat, vest, tie, and deerstalker cap. Fly fishers hire a gillie to show them their beat of a river. The gillie has the last word in a sport that caters to aristocrats and members of powerful wealthy families. On the river the gillie calls all the shots. He chooses the flies and even ties them.

In 1845 Jock, a gillie, and his fishing client Scott were traveling on a boat from England to Norway for a fishing trip. Along the way, Jock tied a huge, colorful salmon fly with toucan feathers, tinsel, and silk. It had very complicated wings made of swan and other feathers.

Today, this concoction is a standard salmon fly known as a Jock Scott. It varies slightly from one tier to the next, and is sometimes made of thirty or more materials. Here are the basic twenty ingredients of a more modest version:

Black, pre-waxed thread
Fine oval silver tinsel
Golden pheasant crest and Indian crow
Black ostrich herl
Golden yellow floss
Toucan feathers
Speckled Guinea fowl
White-tipped turkey tail
Peacock sword
Peacock wing
Yellow, scarlet, and blue swan
Speckled bustard
Florican bustard
Golden pheasant tail
Teal and black-barred woodcock
Brown mallard
Jungle cock
Blue chatterer
Golden pheasant crest
Blue and yellow macaw

In the nineteenth century, there were more ornate and complicated flies than the Jock Scott, but it kicked off the competitive fly-tying tradition. It must have caught salmon because fishers deeply believed in it. However, the Jock Scott is an excellent example of how different a fly looks to the fisher compared to the fish. A dry Jock Scott tied to a leader is a dazzling, bright object, but when wet, it is much duller, with muted colors. And since fish view it from below, it looks far less showy than it does when viewed from the side.

Thousands of wild and gaudy Jock Scotts were tied. They defined salmon fishing in Europe. Nineteenth-century English guidebooks to Norwegian rivers suggesting using different flies for different runs, but a Jock Scott was listed as the first or second choice for almost every run.

The great champion of the elaborate, flashy fly that came to be known as the classic salmon fly was George Mortimer Kelson. Born in 1835, he was a wealthy aristocrat who spent his life largely focused on the kinds of sports that gentlemen pursue, such as steeplechase riding and cricket. He was even a celebrated amateur cricketer. But in time, he grew increasingly interested in fly-tying and became a leading promoter, almost a guru, of classic salmon flies. His 1895 book *The Salmon Fly: How to Dress It and How to Use It* became the bible of the genre.

Kelson claimed to have developed his flies through "science" (curiously, he put the word in quotation marks). He plunged into rivers with flies to see what they looked like from the salmon's point of view. He spent so much time underwater that some said he lost some of his hearing. He also insisted that salmon were attracted to certain colors in certain situations (many have since doubted this). He preached symmetry and balance, while admitting that at times a salmon will bite on most anything. This was why, according to Kelson, bad flies sometimes worked.

Pet theories are an affliction of fly fishers. When to use large flies and when to use small, when dark and when light—this kind of advice is offered in hundreds of books that agree on little except the need for the fly to get in the water and the need for the fishers not to fall in.

But none suffered from this disorder more than Kelson, who had endless theories about flies. Gold tinsel works best in the afternoon, and large flies work best in cold weather, he said. He could tell you when to use flies with white wings, and which colors worked for which rivers. Kelson's theories began with phrases like "it is obvious" or "it barely needs to be stated."

He strongly encouraged the use of exotic feathers and was particularly fond of both blue and red macaw feathers. But he also loved the banded blue chatterer, a stunning blue-and-plum South American bird that is now near extinction, the Nankeen night heron from Southeast Asia, and the ibis. He discouraged the use of dyed common feathers, saying they just were not the same color as the real feathers of exotic birds. He seemed to honestly believe that salmon would care about the difference. He also encouraged using a wide variety of flies because he believed it was a mistake to let a salmon see the same fly too much. He said the Jock Scott was the one exception to this rule. He gave great detail for tying some three hundred elaborate flies—instructions carefully studied by turn-of-the-century salmon anglers.

Even in the early years of the flashy classic salmon fly, America had its doubters. Charles Lanman, a writer who ventured so deep into Canada that some of the rivers he fished did not yet have recognized names, wrote in 1847, "Our books tell us that a gaudy fly is commonly the best killer, but our own experience inclines us to the belief, that a large brown or black hackle, or any neatly made gray fly, is much preferable to the finest fancy specimens."

Elaborate flies tied with expensive feathers were too costly for many American fly fishers, and so they often made do with fur from pet dogs, bears, sometimes even sweaters. Fishers who

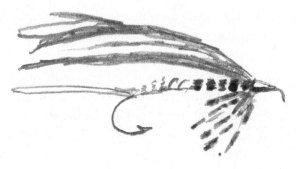

Jock Scott fly

were hunters also had deer, elk, and hare fur at their disposal. And when using these materials, they discovered something surprising. Salmon went for these flies as often as they went for the grand ones. Nonetheless, even in America, the Jock Scott still triumphed. In her 1892 book *Favorite Flies and Their Histories*, the American writer Mary Orvis Marbury wrote, "The Jock Scott seems to arouse the enthusiasm of every one who writes or speaks of it."

In the beginning of the twentieth century, conservation measures and international agreements put an end to much of the exotic feather trade. The Revenue Act of 1913 that lowered tariffs and reestablished the federal income tax also banned the importation of feathers to the United States. In 1921 Britain passed the Importation of Plumage Interdiction Act against the trade in endangered species, which made many of the materials previously used by fly-tiers unavailable and in some cases illegal.

The Jock Scott is one of the few big, gaudy nineteenth-century flies still used today. Others include the silver doctor, red doctor, and green highlander, the latter an 1885 fly first used on the River Ness in Scotland. There are only a few fly-tiers left who know how to tie these complicated patterns, and most of the old classic salmon flies still around are displayed on walls.

Flies do not menace only birds, but also animals, as fur is often used in fly-tying. Fur from the tail of a male deer is easily available, but seal fur, and in particular baby seal fur, once a basic fly-tying material, is rare and its use, illegal.

Synthetic fur and feathers are often used to make flies today, and I suspect that the fish don't mind. Dyed chicken feathers have replaced the feathers of the brilliant orange cock-of-the-rock, which, like the South American rainforests in which it lives, is becoming increasingly rare. Pheasant feathers dyed scarlet have replaced the bright red and yellow feathers of the Indian crow, a South American bird that is not really a crow.

IN 2009 A twenty-year-old American musician, Edwin Rist, broke in through the window of the Natural History Museum at Tring in Hertfordshire, England. The security there was not particularly tight because the museum curators thought that their prized collection, although of great historic value, was not of significant monetary value. The collection contained old, exotic, long-dead birds, acquired during some of the most important biological expeditions of the nineteenth century, including those of Charles Darwin. When the young thief was apprehended, he explained that he was a fly fisherman who had wanted some of the birds' exotic feathers to make rarified salmon flies. The more he explained, the more interested law enforcement became in his personality. He was diagnosed with Asperger's syndrome and because of that diagnosis, was not sentenced to any jail time.

Kirk Wallace Johnson, who wrote a book about this case, *The Feather Thief*, found it difficult to be sure if Rist really had Asperger's Syndrome or was just trying to fool the law, and later many people concluded the latter. He was just a thief who had broken in for profit, they said. It had come out that Rist sold in small amounts to people in the fly-tying trade. The feathers he had stolen from the museum were worth some four hundred thousand dollars, and by the time he was caught, he had already sold some at considerable profit. Many were never recovered.

It probably had never occurred to Rist that if he started talking about flies, he would be spared a prison sentence. He was just talking flies the way many fly fishers do. His level of obsession is not unusual and is generally not thought to be a clinical disorder. Some people are just crazy for flies.

ONE OF THE last great classic salmon fly-tiers, Megan Boyd, died in Scotland in 2001 at the age of eighty-six. Technically she was English, born in Surrey, England, in 1915, but moved to Scotland at the age of three. Her father was the water bailiff, the man who intercepts poaching and code violations, on the River Brora that runs from Loch Brora to the North Sea, a great salmon run strewn with rocks, swift rapids and deep pools. Bob Trussler, a friend of her father who was the keeper of a nearby estate, started teaching her how to tie flies when she was a child and, according to legend, by age twelve she tied flies good enough to sell and went to London with the money to buy her father a suit.

In the 1930s, Boyd moved into a rustic estate cottage that was given to her rent-free for life. And so she never moved.

The cottage had no running water and only got electricity in the 1980s. She tied flies for fifty years at a small kidney-shaped dressing table in her garage by the light of a gas lamp, with a view of the gray North Sea out her window.

Boyd was a classic eccentric, prone to wearing men's tweeds and cutting her own hair. On special occasions she would don a tie decorated with flies. She drove at dangerous speeds down the narrow roads of Sutherland, Scotland, in her 1944 Austin, equipped with running boards and spoke wheels. But she declined to travel to London when Queen Elizabeth II tried to give her the British Empire Medal because she did not want to leave her little dog, Punch.

For nearly sixty years, until her eyes became too weak, Boyd tied for both salmon fishers and collectors who bought her flies to mount on display. She had no telephone, but she received orders through a steady stream of letters and visitors and the occasional urgent telegram. She had piles of such letters from all over the world stacked at an end of her work table. Yet despite the great demand for her flies, she sold them for one to two pounds, or a little over three dollars, at the most. It irritated her when people told her she could charge much more.

Prince Charles was a great admirer of her flies and was seen in his perfectly polished shoes and meticulously tailored sporting clothes seated on a rickety chair in her ramshackle cottage. It is not certain what they were discussing, since Megan had little to say about fishing, an activity she never engaged in and for which she had little interest. Perhaps they talked about her favorite fly, the Popham, a particularly complicated concoction invented in mid-nineteenth-century England.

Megan Boyd and dog Punch

Boyd was generally at least three years behind in orders, but she tried to favor her regular customers. When bad eyesight finally forced her to stop tying in 1988, she still had back orders dating to 1973. Today anyone lucky enough to have a Megan Boyd fly would not fish with it because it is far too valuable to risk losing to a pesky salmon.

Fishers who have used Boyd's flies in the past swear that they magically attracted salmon. Are salmon lovers of beauty? Perhaps. Megan was an artist and often stated that her only motivation was creating something beautiful. I have seen some of the great classic flies of nineteenth-century Ireland and Scotland, but I do not think I have ever seen flies more beautiful than those of Megan Boyd.

She did not use exotic feathers, which by her time would have been illegal and politically unacceptable. She was an active

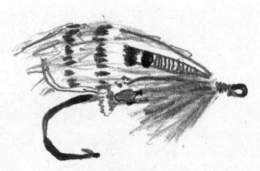

Megan Boyd fly

environmentalist, especially involved with groups dedicated to saving the Atlantic salmon. She scoured the northern Highlands for material. Her flies show a color palette worthy of Matisse and have remarkable balance. The wings of her flies swoop up in a perfect mirror of the downward crook of her hook. The tail is in balance with the head. Everything is in perfect proportion.

Does that perfect balance matter to a fish looking up at a fly from below? What do colors matter once they have become dark and wet? What did Megan care? She was pleased when fishers, especially locals, said they had success fishing with her flies, but all she really wanted was to create beautiful objects.

FLIES CHANGE WITH the culture and politics of the times, despite the fact that the fish themselves never seem to change. They like twenty-first-century flies no more and no less than the flies of any other century. Flies are designed to please humans, not fish.

One nineteenth-century development that has probably not pleased trout but has given fly fishers, including myself, enormous pleasure is the invention of the dry fly. The idea is a simple one, though it was slow to catch on. Trout often feed in the water where we don't see them, and that is the situation for which the traditional fly, or wet fly, was designed. But every now and then a trout rises out of the water to eat an insect floating on the surface and that is the situation for which the dry fly was invented.

It is not certain who invented dry fly fishing, but Frederic Halford, a wealthy English fisher of chalk streams, developed and promoted the idea. He was born into a family of German Jewish textile manufacturers who had changed their last name from Hyman and grown rich in the British midlands. Halford never fly fished until 1868, when he was twenty-four years old and a friend gave him a free beat on the River Wandle. At the time there were a few fishers experimenting with dry flies, but Halford took the idea—then considered a crackpot notion—and transformed it into a popular elite form of fly fishing by developing new flies, casting techniques, and floating lines; carefully studying insects; and spreading the word about the virtues of dry-fly fly fishing through his books. Thanks to him, dry-fly fishing is now a major branch of fly fishing.

By chance, Halford met George Selwyn Marryat in a Winchester tackle shop when he was first starting out, and Marryat helped him develop the dry-fly technique and publish his 1886 *Floating Flies and How to Dress Them*, though only Halford's name appears on the book's cover. Three years later, in the wake of the book's enormous success, Halford, then age

EXPERT DRY FLY-CASTING ON THE STREAM
(*Pencil Portrait of Mr. George La Branche*)

Louis Rhead (American, 1857–1926), Expert Dry Fly-Casting on the Stream

forty-five, left his family's textile business to become a full-time fly fishing author.

Halford's book was discovered by Theodore Gordon, an autodidact who had read the work of Thaddeus Norris, the father of American fly fishing. Originally from the South, Gordon had moved to New York's Catskills Mountains and become a reclusive fisherman. He was fishing in the 1880s, a critical period for Catskill anglers, as the native brook trout were dying out and being replaced by brown trout, which were much more selective about their flies. The old brook trout flies just weren't working anymore and Gordon was searching for new ideas. Noticing that the brown trout were apt to take insects hatching on the surface of the water, he wrote to Halford to learn more about dry-fly fishing. Halford not only sent him information, but sample flies.

Gordon found Halford's flies ill-suited for American rivers and trout, however, and modified them. Wet flies had gone through a similar evolution when transferred from British rivers to American ones. Floating a fly on the rough churning surface of a Catskill river requires a lighter fly than the one required on calm English streams. Gordon designed his own American dry flies, the most famous of which is the Quill Gordon. This is a very delicate, light fly made of a stripped feather quill. It doesn't really look like an insect, but has a way of floating downstream that very much resembles the drift of an insect. The Quill Gordon is one of a number of Gordon's flies still commonly used today. He created American dry-fly fishing in the Catskills' rivers—the Beaverkill, the Neversink, and others—and although he generally shunned social contact, he was a surprisingly good-humored writer whose articles in journals such as *Fishing Gazette* made dry-fly fishing popular in the United States.

In the early twentieth century, the use of dry flies spread to Atlantic salmon fishing. Gordon had talked about using dry flies on the Restigouche River in Canada as early as 1903, and in more recent times, Lee Wulff claimed that a salmon would always take a dry fly if the water temperature was above forty-five degrees. But skepticism on salmon dry flies has always remained. I myself was a doubter until I landed a large chum with a dry fly on Russia's Ozernaya River, though admittedly that is a river where anything is possible.

I must also admit that, like many others, I prefer dry-fly fishing to wet-fly fishing. Unlike the wet fly that drifts out of sight beneath the water's surface, the dry fly is clearly visible, and when it catches a fish's attention, the fish can be seen following it down the river. Will it go for the fly or will it detect the scam? I wonder. The fish gets closer. Then its nose rises out of the water as it goes for the fly, mouth open. It might still change its mind at the last moment—or, it might take the fly, resulting in a furious tug on the line. With a wet fly, the catch begins with the tug, but with a dry fly, it begins as soon as it lands on the water. The entire process can be watched.

Halford turned dry-fly fishing into a cult. He called dry-fly fishers "ultrapurists" and urged everyone to become one. Dry-fly fishing requires more skill than wet-fly fishing. A dry-fly cast must be near perfect to work, and the dry fly must gently float down to the water before the leader lands.

This idea of the superiority of dry-fly fishing to wet-fly fishing spread from Britain to America. In *A River Runs Through It*, Norman Maclean writes of his father's religious education: "He told us about Christ's disciples being fishermen, and we were left to assume, as my brother and I did, that all first-class fishermen on the Sea of Galilee were fly fishermen and that John, the favorite, was a dry fly fisherman."

FLY-TIERS HAVE LARGELY focused on making imitation caddis flies, mayflies, stone flies, true flies, and alder flies. And all these flies have numerous life cycles to imitate. The mayfly lives most of its life underwater as a nymph, so in addition to making artificial adult mayflies, fly-tiers also make imitation nymphs, which are played underwater as opposed to on a river's surface. Every May the nymph swims to the surface, shucks its covering, spreads out its wings, and flies off to the wooded lands along the riverbanks. In this phase it is called a dun and there are many dun flies, the earliest of which was described in the fifteenth-century *Treatyse*.

Flies have remained geographically specific. All Scottish rivers have their own flies, as do many rivers or at least regions in the world. In America there are Maine, Catskills, Pennsylvania, Rocky Mountain, and Oregon flies, along with many others, and what is used in one region is generally not used in another. The fluffy black mite, which I have often used in Idaho, is a western favorite, while the Parmachenee Belle is a Maine original. With its yellow body, red-and-white tail, tall red-and-white wings, and red hackles, the Parmachenee was originally created by Henry P. Wells to fish in Parmachenee Lake but is now widely used throughout Maine.

Many fishers—and disturbingly, some of the most experienced ones—say that too much is made of flies, that if the fish are ready to bite, they will bite at most anything. But many other fishers reject this piscatorial puritanism for a simple reason: they enjoy tying and owning many different flies. It is important to remember that most flies are named after the tiers who invented them, not after the insects they are supposed to resemble.

Quill gordon fly

7

The Comfort of My Rod

We took rod in hand and sallied into the country, as stark mad as was ever Don Quixote from reading books of chivalry.

—WASHINGTON IRVING, "THE ANGLER," IN *THE SKETCH BOOK OF GEOFFREY CRAYON, GENT.*, 1819–20

When Washington Irving compares the fishermen charging a stream with rods in hand to Don Quixote and his lance, the symbol of well-intentioned futility, in the above quote, it is not whimsy. He describes holding a rod and a basket, dressed in leather and, as he mockingly puts it, wearing a coat "perplexed with half a hundred pockets." He continues, "Thus harnessed for the field, he was as great a matter of stare and wonderment among the country folk, who had never seen a regular angler, as was the steel-clad hero of La Mancha among the goatherds of the Sierra Morena."

First and foremost among those leading the futile charge to the stream is the knight's lance, the rod. Since effective fly fishing is all about good casting, the rod, which plays a central role in executing that cast, is critical.

The rod also has a metaphorical importance. It leads the attack. It is the lance, or the spear, or the staff. It is why Captain Benteen charged the Nez Perce with his fishing rod. Gao Xingjian, the first Chinese writer to win the Nobel Prize in Literature, wrote a short story, "Buying a Fishing Rod for My Grandfather," in which the narrator purchases the latest ten-piece fiberglass rod. This rod, which he safely tucks away so that no children will break it, is a resurrection of his grandfather, who had everything taken away from him in the Cultural Revolution. The narrator then searches for his childhood home, but all the houses, the entire neighborhood of traditional homes that he once knew, have been replaced with modern houses. He cannot even find the street on which he lived. The pond where his grandfather fished is also gone. It has been drained and filled in. Finally we learn that even his grandfather is gone, that he died some time ago. All that there is now is this never-used fishing rod.

IN ANCIENT TIMES, a fishing rod was simply a stick with a line tied to one end of it—just as it was for me in my childhood. We do not know much else about ancient fishing rods. The Roman Claudius Aelianus, was the first to give a rod's measurement—six feet—which is short by later standards.

It is not clear of what material these early stubby rods were fashioned. Aelianus mentioned using cornel, which is of the dogwood family. Others of his era made rods of various sturdy reeds, but not bamboo, since it was not available in the ancient Mediterranean world.

In the Middle Ages, as casting became more important, rods became much longer, which meant that lines did, too. The fifteenth-century *Treatyse* states, "If you want to be crafty in angling, you must first learn to make your tackle, that is your rod, your lines of different colors." The writer went on to specify that the rod should be cut from a hazel, aspen, or willow tree between Michaelmas and Candlemas, meaning between September 29, the beginning of autumn, and February 2, supposedly the anniversary of Jesus's presentation at the Temple. The wood was said to be at its strongest during this time. The cut piece was to be a fathom and a half long, meaning nine feet, and "as thick as a man's arm." Then work would begin on this considerable limb:

> Soak it in a hot oven, and set it straight. Then let it cool and dry for a month. Then take and tie it tight with a cockshoot cord, and bind it to a bench or a perfectly square timber. Then take a plumbers wire that is smooth and straight and sharp at one end. And heat the sharp end in a charcoal fire till it is white hot, and then burn the staff through with it, always straight in the pith at both ends, till the holes meet. And after that burn it in the lower end with a spit for roasting birds, and with other spits, each larger than the last, and always the largest last, so that you make your hole always taper-wax. There let it lie still and cool for two days. Untie it then and let it cool in a house-roof in the smoke until it is thoroughly dry. In the same season, take a fair rod of green hazel, and soak it even and straight, and let it dry with the staff. And to make

the upper half of the upper section, take a fair shoot of black thorn, crabtree, medlar or juniper, cut in the same season and well soaked and straightened, and bind them together neatly so that the upper section may go exactly into the above mentioned hole. Then shave your staff down and make a taper-wax. Then ferrule the staff at both end with long hoops of iron or latten in the neatest manner, with a spike in the lower end fastened with a running device for pulling your upper section in and out. Then set your upper section a hand breath inside the upper end of your staff in such a way that it may be as big there as in any other place above. Then with a cord of six hairs, strengthen your upper section at the upper end as far down as the place where it is tied together; and arrange the cord neatly and tie it firmly on the top, with a loop to fasten your fishing line on.

So, this rod is made up of several pieces, like fishing rods today. Since the length of the extensions is not given, the total length of the rod is not certain, but it appears to be about eighteen feet long, a very long rod.

While the *Treatyse* describes this rod as being light and very nimble, it is an extremely heavy rod by today's standards. And so it is not surprising that Europeans used two-handed casts. It would be nearly impossible to cast this rod with one hand. This rod is also clearly not intended for a woman angler—another argument against the Dame Juliana myth. Even for a large man, a day spent casting with this rod would be exhausting.

Fashioning a rod of this type, and probably fly fishing in general, must have been the prerogative of the leisure class. If you chose your log around Michaelmas and worked diligently, employing the skills of a cabinet maker, blacksmith, and metal worker, drying, smoking, boring; you might have a good rod by the opening of the trout season the following spring. It still had the line tied off the tip of the rod.

In 1614 Gervase Markham gave this almost equally complicated formula for fashioning a rod out of elm or hazel wood:

> For the choice then of your angle-rod, some anglers are of the opinion that the best should be composed of two pieces, a main body and a small pliant top. The main body would be of a fine grown ground-witchen or a ground-elm of at least nine or ten feet in length, straight, smooth, without knots and differing much at either end in substance or thickness. It would be gathered at the fall of the leaf and laid up in some place where it may lie straight and self-season; for to bake them in the fire, when they are green is not so good, but after they are well dried and have self-seasoned then bake them in the fire and set them so straight that even an arrow cannot surpass them, is excellent; then you may take the upper rind and what with the smoke and their age, their colour will be so dark that they will not reflect into the water, which is the principal observation. Your rod having been made straight and seasoned, you shall, the upper end thereof, with an augur or hot iron, a hot iron is better, burn a hole, about three inches deep and a finger wide. Then on the outside of the rod, from the top of the hole to the bottom, you shall wrap it about with either strong double twisted thread, well waxed or pitched, or with shoemakers' thread doubled many times and well waxed with shoemakers' wax and the last end fastened under the last fold, so closely

that it does not loosen: this will keep the rod from cleaving or breaking where the hollow was made.

Having made the stock, fix the top into the hole, which would be very small ground-hazel, growing upwards from the earth, very smooth and straight, which would be cut at the latter end of the year and lie in season all winter, the upper rind by no means being taken off, neither rod put into the fire but only seasoned in a dry place, where it may lie straight and have both wind and some air from the fire to reach it. This top must be pliant and bending, yet of such sufficient strength that it will not break with any reasonable jerk, but if it is bent in any way will return to its former straightness. This top-wand would be a yard and half, or an ell [forty-five inches] at least in length, and the smallest end would be fastened with a wrap of hair, a strong loop of hair, about an inch long, to which you may at pleasure fasten your fishing line: and the bigger end of the top must be thrust into the socket of the stock and made so fast that it does not loosen nor shake out with any shaking or other reasonable violence.

This was an attempt at making a springier, more buoyant rod, known in fishing parlance as a rod with good "action." But by the Elizabethan age, Markham's time, professional rod-builders were already at work, and Markham's advice, despite the detailed directions he gives above, was that fishers buy rather than make their rods. He wrote, "There is a great choice of them in every haberdashery shop."

If there was a wide selection of fly fishing rods in every haberdashery shop in England, or even just in London, fly fishing had become far more popular by then than it had been in the time of the *Treatyse*. The author of the *Treatyse* wrote that you could walk down the street with a fishing rod and no one would guess for what it was going to be used.

Though seventeenth-century rods were far heavier than we use today, the fishermen knew how to play a fish on a fly rod the same way we do. Robert Venables fished with a rod of blackthorn made with a center piece of cane and a tip of whale baleen. This was not an unusual rod for the period. He emphasized that the rod had to be well tapered so that it would bend well. "The equal bending of the rod saveth the line," he wrote, and this principle endures today on modern rods. When a fish is on the line, the rod must be held high, and vertically, so that it bends in an arch. This takes stress off the line and prevents the rod from snapping. A rod that doesn't bend could easily snap.

In his 1653 book Thomas Barker said that a rod must be "light and tender," and emphasized the importance of a good taper: "The first thing you must gaine is a neat taper. Rod, light before and with a tender hazel top, which is very gentle." By "gentle" he meant supple, given to bending, and the point of having the lower part "light" (though by modern standards, this was never achieved in Barker's time) was to make casting easier.

In the seventeenth and eighteenth centuries, the golden age of whaling, rod tips were made of baleen, a natural filter found in the mouths of certain whales with no teeth, including the minke, bowhead, blue, gray, and humpback. It serves as a screen for the whales when they are collecting krill, shrimp, and plankton for food. Baleen made the rod's tip considerably lighter than the rest of the rod, was strong and did not easily break, and gave the rod better balance by keeping most of its weight in its lower part.

Rods specifically made for fly fishing did not exist until the mid 1700s. Fishing rods were for all kinds of fishing but then fly fishers started thinking that certain characteristics of lightness and limberness would be better suited for fly fishing. Once rods became more specialized, a trout rod was different than a salmon rod. Both were long by modern standards; a trout rod was twelve feet or more. Twelve feet is usually as long as a trout rod gets today. Salmon rods were seventeen feet or longer, which would be very long today. Different woods were used. Some fishers liked ash, pine, or willow. Some liked heavier and some liked lighter. By 1750 fly fishermen who made their own rods were extremely rare. They were all following Markham's advice and heading to the haberdashery, though by then it was the tackle shop.

The British became rod and rod materials exporters, mainly to their colonies. Americans were now building their own rods, but with the import of British materials, those rods changed. Imported greenheart and lancewood were coming in and sometimes replacing American hickory and hazel. An even bigger change was, the arrival of Calcutta cane.

According to legend, British officers had started taking bamboo lances back to England as souvenirs in the 1700s. Some of these lances were used as fishing rods, while others, broken into smaller pieces, became favored as rod tips. There were regular knots in the bamboo that kept it from being a clean rod, however, and so rod-makers started cutting the bamboo into strips with beveled edges and gluing them together. Thomas Aldred of London claimed that he made the first split-cane rod in 1851, but his and other early attempts were crude, simply three long strips glued together. The Americans saw a greater potential for bamboo.

Bamboo is a subfamily of ninety-one genera and about one thousand species of grass. It is the most numerous group of grasses and grows in many different climates. yet is not native to many of the important fly fishing regions of the world. The bamboo's vertical stalks, called culms, are jointed, which is characteristic of grasses, though most are too small for this to be evident. The culms' interior is soft and spongy, but its joints, called nodes, are fairly solid dividers. Furthermore, the culms are composed of bundles of vertical tubes held together with lignin, a natural polymer found in most cellulose cells. These tubes are encased in a hard exterior. The cellulose tubing nearest the exterior is particularly dense and this material, along with the plant's harder outer shell, is what is used to make split-cane rods. Bamboo's combination of light weight, strength, and flexibility make it an ideal substance for fishing rods. Also, unlike many other rod materials, cane does not continue to vibrate after a cast is completed, making it less tiring to use.

In about 1862, Samuel Phillippe, a Pennsylvania gun-maker, built an entire rod out of four strips of split cane. Later, Solon Phillippe, son of Samuel, and Charles Murphy and E. A. Green, both New Jersey rod-makers, also started splitting cane to make rods. Thaddeus Norris also did the same. Murphy sold a number of four-strip rods in New York, and after 1864 may have been the first to start making six-strip rods. The added strips gave the rod better action.

Six strips of bamboo, triangularly shaped to fit together, glued and wrapped with silk thread, produced a tapered hexagonal rod. It was lighter, stronger, and more flexible than any rod in history. To plane the triangular strips in such a way that they fit together was a demanding, time-consuming task, but when done well, it produced the best fly rod anyone had seen. Other times it was a disaster. The results were not predictable.

Then came Hiram Leonard from Bangor, Maine, sometimes called the "father of bamboo rods." Like most people anointed as the father of some aspect of fly fishing, he was a perfecter, not an originator. Also, like many of the nineteenth-century American rod-builders, he was a gun-maker. He made musical instruments, too, and invented a machine for beveling bamboo strips that could produce far more perfectly tapered rods in much less time than had been done before. In 1876 his company,

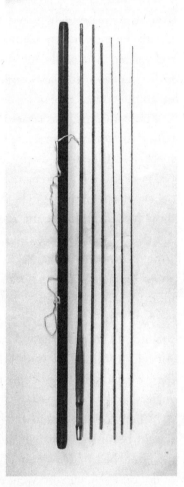

Thaddeus Norris, fishing rod, nineteenth century

the H.L. Leonard Rod Company, produced about two hundred rods with only eleven employees. Leonard was very secretive, however, and so it took time for other rod-makers to learn his techniques.

One of Leonard's secrets was his discovery of a better cane, Tonkin cane, which grows in only a small area north of Guangdong (formerly Canton Province), China. Previously, rod-makers had used cane from Kolkata (formerly Calcutta), India. Leonard may have originally switched to Tonkin because of a supply problem. For a time, Tonkin cane, which is smooth and unblemished, was treated with acid to look more like the better known and appreciated Calcutta cane, which has brown speckles. but he soon discovered that Tonkin is straighter than Calcutta and its outer enamel harder. Today, many others also believe that Tonkin is the better bamboo for rod-making even though the softer Calcutta is easier to work with. Tonkin was difficult to obtain after the Chinese Revolution, but in the 1980s, became easily available again.

As Leonard's secrets became understood by others in the industry, split-cane rods became a common commercial product. For a time, too, they were a distinctly American product. Even the British started using them, although in the American style they were usually single-handed, rather than the two-handed Spey type preferred by European salmon anglers.

When making a split-cane rod, the rod's middle section should be only about half the weight of its butt end and its tip should be half the weight of its middle section. This tapering of not only size but also weight can create a perfectly balanced rod. Another part of the formula is the glue. It should be heated, and the bamboo submerged in it and then dried. But how hot should the glue be? How long should the bamboo be submerged? And how long should it dry? Some say a year. Also, what kind of glue is best? Some use ordinary glue, some gelatin sold in grocery stores, some isinglass made from fish bladders.

In addition, a craftsman needs to carefully select the best culms of bamboo for his rod. Brown areas on culms indicate the beginning of rot, and indentations in the nodes are an undesirable mark. The rod-maker needs to work with the straightest and smoothest culms possible.

The demands of rod-making, and the ever-present possibility of making a better rod than has ever been made before, cause some rod-makers to become even more obsessed than fly-tiers. Fishers thus afflicted often abandon fly-tying in preference for rod-making, because you can buy excellent flies but you can't buy rods as perfect as the ones you can make yourself if you are a great craftsman. Fly fishers who do not make their own rods tend to become consumed with rods, too. As Thaddeus Norris said back in 1864, "Anglers are apt to become fastidious as to the spring and taper of their rods, especially those used for fly fishing."

Edmund Everett Garrison, born in Yonkers, New York, in 1893, is remembered as one of the great rod-builders. He was a structural engineer who built rods during the evenings and on weekends. As he worked, he developed equipment and ideas for producing better split-cane rods, and after retiring from engineering, worked as a rod-builder full time. Like fly-tier Megan Boyd, he could never keep up with demand. His original rods cost forty-five dollars, but in later years they were valued in the thousands of dollars. In a typical year, Garrison made about twenty-five rods, but one year he made forty rods to earn enough money for a down payment on a new house. He tested his new rods by casting them on his lawn, and sometimes rejected them. By the time of his death in 1975, he had made 650 rods, which may not sound like a lot; but considering the time, care, and skill that went in to each one, it is a substantial number.

Hoagy B. Carmichael, an avid fly fisherman, met Garrison in 1966, studied his work closely, and became a leading split-cane rod-maker himself. Hoagy B. is the son of Hoagy Carmichael, the songwriter with fifty hits to his name, including "Georgia on My Mind," "The Nearness of You," and "Stardust." He was featured as the piano player in a number of prominent Hollywood movies, so his son grew up in Hollywood knowing movie stars. Hoagy the father did not fish, but he loved golf and taught his son the game. Yet Hoagy B. had a secret longing. When he was eight years old, he had a subscription to *Outdoor Life* magazine and would look at pictures of fishing lures under the covers in his bed at night when he was supposed to be sleeping. "I loved the lures," he said. It was the beginning of his lifelong love of fishing tackle.

During Hoagy's childhood, a movie theater in Hollywood had a boys' special featuring short Westerns on Saturdays. The boys would attend in their cowboy outfits, with cap guns. Not far away was Kerr's, a sporting goods shop frequented by movie stars. Some of those stars, such as Clark Gable and Gary Cooper, were genuine fishermen, but others stopped by just to pose. There was a publicity shot of Ava Gardner casting. No one has ever looked better in waders, but a close examination of the picture showed her fly was stuck from the backcast in the back of her waders.

Hoagy visited Kerr's once or twice after the movies, and when he got a little older, biked there to look at the tackle. But no one ever took him fishing.

As an adult, Hoagy moved to New York City and became a Wall Street broker. He took a trip to Expo 67 in Montreal with his girlfriend, who happened to be a fly fisher. On the way back they stopped at the famous Battenkill River in Vermont. She caught browns and brookies. He caught nothing. But a durable love affair was cemented—not with the girl (they broke up soon afterward), but with fly fishing. He moved to Boston to produce films and fished the Battenkill on weekends. And has been fishing it ever since.

The Battenkill is a tough but beautiful river. Its banks are heavily overgrown with trees and bushes, and the river seems to whisper through a green tunnel. When the water is low, there is only a slight riffle to the glass-like surface as the water makes its way silently downstream. The trout, browns and brook, will occasionally leap up to grab an insect. But these are educated fish. The Battenkill has been thoroughly fished for a long time and since fishers are required to release their

Battenkill River, Vermont, home to brook and brown trout

catch, the fish know a fake fly when they see one. Some people even think the current generations of trout, especially browns, may have adapted genetically to fishers so that they instinctively know how to deal with their tricks. Avoiding fishers seems to be one of their survival skills.

Hoagy became a fly fishing expert and even wrote a two-volume history of the Grand Cascapédia River in Quebec, one of the great Atlantic salmon fly fishing rivers. He also became a high-quality split-cane rod-builder whose rods sell for ten thousand dollars each, a top priced rod, though a Garrison rod, if you can find one, goes for fifteen thousand dollars. Hoagy once needled me, saying, "How come you don't fish with bamboo, are you too cheap?"

He was joking, but it is true, I am cheap. When you are fighting to land a big strong fish, one that is forcing your rod up high and doubling over its tip, your rod is at risk. I have never broken a rod, but it can easily happen. So while you are fighting the fish, it is nice to know that your rod is not worth ten thousand dollars.

Through his books and films he has promoted rod-building, and there are more split-cane rod-builders than ever. But the production is very small and most of the rod-builders are curious individualists. Philipp Sicher in Switzerland has made more than seventy rods. His rods have the distinction of a fingerprint of the rod owner in mother-of-pearl on the bottom of the butt end. Sicher has made rods with only four and five strips but also six and eight, and he even made a twelve-strip rod.

For a time, Hoagy was ill and could not go fishing. He confided to me that he did not miss standing in the river or the pull of a fish on the line. "What I fantasized about was putting all my tackle in my car, driving up to the Battenkill,

Hoagy Carmichael building a split-cane rod

spreading out the tackle, holding the rod, checking the leader, seeing what flies I have—I'm interested in tackle."

IN THE TWENTIETH century, a number of new types of rods were developed. Among them were solid steel rods and their lighter cousins, hollow steel rods. Steel rods can have very good action and are extremely strong, but they vibrate after a fly lands, which is a problem. Vibration makes casting very tiring, especially at the end of a long day. I also wonder what impact a rod's vibration has on fish. Fish perceive sound as vibrations and are very sensitive to them.

In 1947 fiberglass rods came into use. They were solid at first, but by the 1950s, hollow fiberglass rods had become very popular. Lee Wulff was a great fan of them. Fiberglass rods are made up of thin glass fibers molded into tapering shells and are extremely elastic, perhaps as elastic as split bamboo, and far easier to make and much cheaper to buy. They can also be made to order according to the length and type of action desired. Once a fisher establishes the characteristics of the rod he or she wants, an infinite number of identical copies can be made.

While working on advanced aircraft design in the late sixties, the Royal Aircraft Establishment at Farnborough in South London discovered a new material called carbon fiber. No one will give any details of how exactly that came about, but I like to think that some aerospace engineer who was also a passionate fly fisher discovered the new material and instantly realized that it would make a great fly fishing rod. In any event, it does.

Carbon rods, which range in price, are considered to be the best rods for the money today. But new ideas for rods are always being tried out. A two-thousand-dollar titanium rod and rods made of boron are among the newest inventions. But for how long?

Then there is always something "new" being rediscovered such as the ancient Japanese tenkara fishing rod—tenkara in Japanese meaning, it is said, "from the heavens." The tenkara rod was developed in the twelfth century, possibly as part of the training of a samurai warrior. The rod seems to have the Zen elements of patience, contemplation, and simplicity. Like a fifteenth-century European rod, it has no reel. The line is simply tied to the end of the rod. Unlike the old European rods, though, the tenkara is lightweight and its line is longer than the length of the rod. In the old European formula the line was the same length as the rod.

The tenkara appeals to purists, the dry-fly type. It is held high so that little of its line goes in the water, forming a direct line from fish to rod tip. There is less line to scare away a fish. When a fish bites, the rod is held even higher and back a bit so that the fisher can reach up, grab the line, and pull in the fish with his hands. There is something very immediate about this.

Originally, tenkara rods were made of bamboo, but they are now made of carbon fiber. They have no line rings and can telescope down into very small sizes that are easily packable in suitcases—the most portable tackle imaginable. Once I was fishing with a tenkara in a national park on an afternoon when I had accidentally let my fishing license expire by one day. A ranger passed by but did not recognize my tenkara as a real fishing rod—and since he said I had no fishing rod, he did not fine me.

I once had a great time catching frisky little cutthroats in the Snake River with a tenkara, but I can't imagine using it to catch a salmon or a big, hard-fighting rainbow because it has no line to run out. Your rod has to be well matched to the fish you are pursuing.

Owl-eye optic fly

8

Send You Reeling

Hark to the music of the reel!
It murmurs and it closes,
Silence falls on the conquering wheel,
The wearied line reposes
No birr! No whir! The salmon's ours:
The noble fish, the thumper!

—THOMAS TOD STODDART, "THE TAKING
OF THE SALMON," 1836

Reels, which figure so prominently in other types of fishing, have always played a minor role in fly fishing, which is why the idea of tenkara fishing with no reel at all does not shock most fly fishers. Originally, and for many centuries, fly rods had no reels.

There are illustrations of fishermen using reels in China in the 1100s, and Joseph Needham's classic *Science and Civilisation in China* suggests that the Chinese may have been using reels as far back as the fourth century. A drawing dated 1255 shows a man fishing off the stern of his boat with a short rod. On its butt end is a round device with a spoke wheel, very much resembling a modern reel. But none of these rods was a fly rod.

Originally, reels seem to have been used more for carrying a supply of line than for actually reeling in a fish. This is still true at times in fly fishing today.

One of the most certain ways to lose a fish is to not let it run. This may cause the fish to break the line or leader or, as with salmon and some other large fish, tear the hook out of its mouth. Before reels, the lengths of lines were limited and it was often not possible to let the fish run unless, as was sometimes suggested, you just threw your rod in the river and let the fish drag it until exhausted. Using a reel with a substantial amount of line on the spool is a much better solution than that. Letting the fish run may also have been one of the original purposes of the reel, as it was first developed for use with large fish such as salmon and pike.

The earliest mention of a reel is in Thomas Barker's work of the mid-seventeenth century. He called the reel a "winder," and wrote of "a wind to turn with a barrel to gather up line." He suggested using the winder when fishing for pike and recommended "winding up your line" when landing salmon. Franck, possibly the first salmon fly fisherman, used a reel, too, but his 1658 book was not published until 1694. Walton does not appear to have used a reel, but in his 1655 edition observes that there were some fishermen who had a wheel at the middle of their rods. A few years later, in 1662, Venables also referred to reels, which he called winches. So the reel appears to have been invented, at least in England, in the 1650s.

The reel was only one of several early solutions for carrying extra line. Thomas Nobbes in his 1682 *The Complete Troller*, a book specifically about bait fishing for pike, said that he wrapped spare line around a ring that he wore for that purpose. Other fishers used various types of spools. The French in the early eighteenth century used a spool held in the left hand containing line that could be played out as needed. Some fishers simply kept a large amount of extra line sitting in the stream behind them, a technique I sometimes use because when a fish runs, I would rather feed it through my fingers than off a reel. In the seventeenth century, some French anglers did the same when they coiled spare line in a basket that floated behind them. The Japanese, when they were not tenkara purists, attached a protrusion to the butt of the rod around which spare line could be wrapped.

The earliest ad for reels for sale appeared in London in 1726 when Charles Kirby, an esteemed hook-maker, advertised that "he selleth also the best sort of winches." His claiming to be the best suggests that by the early eighteenth century, the reel was a recognized item for sale in a tackle shop. The 1760 edition of Walton, included a reel on its list of the twenty-six essentials for fly fishing.

Onesimus Ustonson, who owned a London tackle shop, was the leading reel-maker of the eighteenth century. His heavy solid brass or ivory reels were considered to be the very finest, and he was the outfitter for the royal family as well as for the explorer James Cook. He was also the inventor of the multiplying reel. Although the multiplying reel is often said to be an American invention, his were clearly earlier. Through a complicated rigging system, the spool on this type of reel would turn twice for a single revolution of the crank so that a fish could be pulled in much faster. It is not known how many multiplying reels Ustonson made, but the few that have survived—made of brass and signed with his name—are collectors' items sometimes worth more than ten thousand dollars.

By the eighteenth century, reels, still called winches, had become substantial manufactured devices usually made of solid brass, handsome to look at and heavy to hold. These large reels were not efficient when playing a fish. They often had iron parts and were frequently mounted on rods by means of spikes, which sometimes pulled out while fishing. But they were excellent for storing line.

Reels were made in England for local use and for export to America. Mid-eighteenth-century Boston papers carried ads for imported British reels, and reels were being sold at a store called Pole's in the 1770s. This suggests that they were now a common part of American fishing tackle.

The French developed a reel-like device made of wicker. The British found it ugly and clumsy, but the French found the British brass reel too heavy. As is often the case in Anglo–French disputes, both sides were right.

Before the advent of reels, a line was attached to the tip of a rod with a loop of horsehair. This did not prevent fish from running and taking extra line, however, so an iron ring through which the line could pass soon replaced the horsehair loop.

Now, the line could pass so a reel could be used. But a reel used by itself puts tremendous strain on the tip of a rod, and though there are no clear records on this, I suspect that a lot of rods were split in this way. In the eighteenth century a series of rings was attached along the rod, which alleviated some of the strain, and this is the system still used today. The early rings were simply tacked into the rod, though, and often pulled out. The lines, were made of knotted horsehair, and the knots would often snag in the rings.

IN THE NINETEENTH century, aristocrats commissioned spectacular reels. In 1851 Prince Albert commissioned the London tackle-maker G. Little to make an engraved silver reel with an ivory handle. It was too heavy to balance well and its stubby ivory-handle crank did not reel in strong fish easily, but it was a beautiful object. The British also commissioned very well crafted wooden reels as well, and some of these were used in the United States.

Up until the mid-nineteenth century, Americans used either British tackle or American tackle built according to British design, but about 1850 that changed. Americans started to develop their own ideas and unique tackle. This development started with American rod-builders, but soon spread to reels.

Innovation was occurring in England, too, which might have inspired Americans. The British were losing interest in multiplying reels and began producing a simple single-action reel, which was called the Birmingham reel because many were made in Birmingham, a city of light industry and invention most famously, James Watt's steam engine.

Birmingham reels are sometimes called the first modern reel because they were mass-produced. Unlike the earlier, hand-crafted reels, which had been quirky and individual and

Unknown maker, Dual Use Reel, ca. 1826, 3 inches in diameter

sometimes even signed, the Birmingham reels all looked the same. They were made of brass, had an ivory or horn handle, and included a conventional modern "foot" to attach to the rod.

Another popular nineteenth-century British single-action reel was the Nottingham, which was lighter than the Birmingham because it was made of walnut or mahogany wood. Developed in the city of Nottingham, which is on the River Trent, these reels were first popularized on that river but soon spread throughout England and were even exported to America. Unlike the Birmingham, the Nottingham was a beautiful little machine, but its wood did not hold up well. It often lost its finish and sometimes even split in pieces.

Meanwhile, Americans were making their own reels, in many cases multiplying reels. The famous Kentucky reel, first made in Frankfort, Kentucky, in 1893 was originally for bass fishing. It was made of brass and was quite heavy.

Modern innovation in American reels began with William Billinghurst, a gun-maker and shop owner in Rochester, New York, celebrated for making some of the finest muzzle-loading rifles. During the Civil War, factory-made weapons such as the Colt repeating rifle had begun to dominate the gun industry, and after the war Billinghurst's was one of the few small gun shops to survive. This was partly because he had patented a popular fly reel in 1859. The fourth single-action fly fishing reel developed in America, it was made of two brass-wire concave baskets fitted together. This left the line on the spool exposed to air so that it could dry, an important innovation for silk line. Modern collectors call a Billinghurst reel "a birdcage reel," which is a good description. For a single-action reel, it wound up line with surprising speed. Also, it was mounted sticking out from the reel instead of flat against it, an innovation that would be copied by all subsequent reels.

In 1856 Charles F. Orvis, who had been making solid wooden rods as a hobby, opened a tackle shop in a wood-shingled white house on the Battenkill River in Manchester, Vermont—a store now known as an enduring innovator in the merchandizing of fishing tackle. In 1874 he built a new fly reel that became the prototype for the modern fly reel. Made of German nickel silver with two plates riveted to pillars holding the two sides together, it was mounted standing out from the rod, not flat against it. The plates were perforated, which made the reel lighter and also helped keep the line dry. The spool was narrow and deep so that it could carry a lot of line and not tangle it.

William Billinghurst, Fly Reel, ca. 1865, patented August 9, 1859

The reels came in handsome, hinged walnut boxes and were often cherished and well cared for by their owners. Many are still in good condition today.

Reels have often remained objects of beauty. Sometimes they have names engraved in them. Antique reels can sell to collectors at auctions for as much as ten thousand dollars.

Americans started building lighter reels based on the Orvis model, but only a few modifications, such as attaching the plates to the pillars with screws instead of rivets, were made. One popular variation, made in Maine, was the 1877 Leonard reel. Many later reels have been based on either the Leonard or the Orvis, clearly the most influential of modern reels.

C. F. Orvis Co., Fly Reel, ca. 1880, patented May 12, 1874, 2 7/8 inches diameter

Starting in the 1860s Edward Vom Hofe, a German immigrant, built salmon reels made of hard rubber and nickel silver for use on Canada's Restigouche River. Vom Hofe was also the first to make a lightweight aluminum reel.

An Orvis in its wooden box sold for five dollars in the 1870s, which would be the equivalent of about one hundred twelve dollars today. A top-quality reel was, and still is, expensive. But there were also inexpensive serviceable models available, made by companies such as Meisselbach and Hendryx.

Some of the newest reels are now made of light-weight and durable magnesium, but in general there are few new fly reel inventions because fly fishers, along with most other anglers, do not have a lot of expectations for their reels. Clarence Birdseye, the mid-twentieth-century inventor, famous for developing a technique for deep-freezing foods, held more than three hundred patents, including ones for various lightbulbs and a whale harpoon, but his least successful invention was the Birdseye fishing reel. Watching commercial snapper fishermen in Galveston, Texas, he had had an idea for a reel that enabled a fisherman to throw a switch when a fish bites, and—zzzzwh!—the reel automatically pulled in the line. But even commercial fishermen were not interested in his invention. Hauling out the fish is part of fishing. He did not sell one reel.

Nymph fly

9

A Good Line

Along the silver streams of Tweed,
'Tis blithe the mimic fly to lead,
When to the hook the salmon springs,
And the line whistles through the rings . . .

—SIR WALTER SCOTT, "ON ETTRICK FOREST'S
MOUNTAINS DUN"

For those who love to collect objects, hooks and lines will
never have the sex appeal of flies, rods, and reels. But
nothing has had more variation or been more critical to the
development of fly fishing than the evolution of fishing lines
and hooks.

Today, those obsessed with fly fishing primarily focus on
building rods and tying flies. But there was a time when a fisherman made everything, even lines, leaders, and hooks.

Hooks must have been crude affairs when fishermen made
their own, though a few might have been exquisite. Early fishers
did have the advantage of being able to shape the length and

curve of their hooks exactly to their liking. The fifteenth-century *Treatyse* explained:

> You must understand that the subtlest and hardest art in making your tackle is to make your hooks, for making of which you must have suitable files, thin and sharp and beaten small; a semi-clamp of iron; a bender, a pair of long and small tongs; a hard knife somewhat thick; an anvil; and a little hammer.

There are a lot of variables involved in making a good fishhook. If the point leans toward the shaft, it is less likely that the fish will be hooked, but if it is pointed away from the shaft, the fish can more easily unhook itself. A short-point hook, one with its point formed immediately after the crook in the shaft, will also easily hook a fish but tends to be easier for the fish to unhook. Compromises have to be made. A hookmaker in London during the time of Walton, Cotton, Barker, and Venables, all of whom probably used his hooks, made hooks that were turned out slightly but compensated for this by making bigger bends in their crooks. His hooks were lighter and more durable than earlier hooks, but still had no eyes. Fishers had to tie their lines to the hooks' shafts.

In the 1700s quality steel became available and hooks started to be produced industrially. Eyes made of silkworm gut were added. They turned brittle when dry and rotted when wet, but anglers stuck with them until the mid-nineteenth century. The metal eye at the end of the hook was first made for dry-fly fishers, in 1845. Fly fishers resisted them, however, as they often do with ideas that promise to make fishing easier. There is always the suspicion that using them might be cheating.

Lines were first made of horsehair, preferably from the tail, twisted and knotted. Horsehair could be dyed to match the color of the river at any time of year—brown, green, or russet—and the horsehair line was fashioned the same way the nylon line is fashioned today. It was tapered, becoming ever thinner as it progressed toward the fly, with its final length, to which the fly was attached, so thin that the fish couldn't see it. The thinner the better, therefore, though thinner lines broke more easily and demanded greater skill from anglers landing their fish.

Tapering was accomplished by reducing the number of hairs twisted into the line. A line might start out having as many as eighteen hairs and then tie off in subsequent bundles with fewer and fewer strands until there were only two or three. Barker said that trout could be caught with three hairs on the leader, or end of the line, but more trout could be taken with only one. The single strand would make it easier to deceive the fish but it would take considerable skill to land a trout without breaking the single hair. The trick with any line is to keep the tension so consistent that the fish cannot loop or jerk the line but also loose enough so that the fish, exerting force, will take line and not snap it.

In an earlier time, the *Treatyse* recommended using a single hair for catching minnows, two for roach, slightly more for trout, and up to fifteen for salmon. A fifteen-hair leader might be too thick. Charles Cotton wrote that the leader should be no more than two hairs. "To fish fine and far off is the first principle of trout angling," he said. He also wrote that anyone who could not land a twenty-inch trout (a sizable specimen) with only two hairs "deserves not the name of angler."

Horsehair has good elasticity, so the horsehair lines had a bit of give, needed when fighting large fish; but horsehair is not supple and its stiffness inhibited the flow of a good cast. That same stiffness had advantage, as it kept the lines free of the tangles and snarls that later fishers would experience. In the eighteenth century, line-makers started to weave the hairs rather than knot them in a series of sections, and this enabled the line to glide more smoothly through a ring, facilitating the use of the new invention, reels.

Later, silk strands were added, and then braided silk lines were used, followed by linen lines and cotton lines. Sometimes hemp was also used. The problem with all these lines was that after a short period, an hour at most, they became waterlogged and too heavy to use. Horsehair was more water resistant, and so some continued to fish with it.

While two dyed horsehairs made a fine leader that a fish could not see, in the mid-seventeenth century, Europeans began borrowing from the Chinese and making leaders out of transparent gut. In fact, a leader came to be called a "gut" and the term is still in use even though today's leaders are rarely made of gut. Venables used gut the easy way, by fashioning leaders out of the higher-pitched strings of lutes and other stringed instruments, which were made from sheep or cow intestines, which was misleadingly called catgut. The Swiss and the Northern Italians were said to have the best leaders, because their gut was made from the bellies of silkworms.

In the eighteenth century, gut could be purchased, but the more obsessed fishers added a new dimension to fly fishing mania by raising their own silkworms, curing them in vinegar, and drawing out their guts. In 1920 Dr. George Parker Holden, the great split-cane rod-builder who first interested Garrison in the craft, published *The Idyl of Split-Bamboo*. The book included not only detailed information on bamboo selection, splitting, and rod-making, but also a long section by Edwin T. Wiffen of New Rochelle, New York, on cultivating and drawing out the guts of silkworms.

More developments followed. In the mid-nineteenth century, oil-soaked linen and silk were woven into hollow floating lines. Later, a machine was invented to weave fishing lines out of silk, and such lines were used until the 1930s when DuPont invented nylon. Silk line would float for only about an hour until it became waterlogged, but nylon line was made with a hollow center that kept it afloat and never became waterlogged.

Today, lines and leaders are mostly manufactured out of nylon, but that has by no means made things simpler. The modern fly fisher has many more decisions to make than did the old-time angler dyeing and bundling horsehairs. What kind of taper is best? Should the line be sinking or floating? How light or heavy should the line be? What kind of leader matches what line? The choice of tomorrow morning's fishing line often makes for a long evening conversation.

When I was a child, tying string to a stick, I had no idea how many demands a real fly fisher makes of a line. Explains Roderick Haig-Brown:

> It must be heavy enough to use the action of the rod and carry the fly out accurately to a fair distance; it should be smooth enough not to tangle when looped in the hand; it must be light enough to fall gently near the fly, it must float or sink in accordance with the fisherman's desires and intentions; and it must be adaptable to the various casts

he may wish to make—overhand or underhand, roll or angle, spey or double spey, short or long or in between.

You may fish with a line that is too stiff, a reel that is too slow, a hook that is less than desirable, or a poor selection of flies, but if you do not have a line that will accomplish what Haig-Brown details above, the success of your fishing trip will be in doubt.

Bivisible salmon dry fly

10

Wading In

I waded, deepening, into the dark water.
Evening, and the push
And swirl of the river as it closed
Around my legs and held on.

—RAYMOND CARVER, "THE RIVER"

T he greatest change to come about in fly fishing has been waterproof waders. These allow the fisher to stand waist-high in cold waters and stay dry—and even sufficiently warm, if properly dressed. Without waders an angler might step into a river anyway, as characters do in Hemingway's fiction, but humans cannot endure much more than an hour in most fly fishing rivers.

Look at engravings and drawings of fly fishing from any time before the mid-twentieth century, and you will not see anglers in the water. They are fishing from the riverbanks, sometimes perched on large overhanging rocks in order to cast farther out.

Before waders, there were a variety of wading accoutrements available, most aimed at keeping a fisher's legs dry as long as he or she did not step too far into the river. Among these items were wading stockings, trouting pants, and trouting boots, none of which worked in water much deeper than mid-thigh high. In England upper-class fishermen also had another invaluable piece of equipment: the "gillie wetfoot," or gillie who carried the fisher through the river.

Then came the Europeans' discovery of rubber, long used by the South Americans, who harvested it from the hevea tree that grew wild in the rain forests. According to legend, and possibly true, Christopher Columbus introduced Europeans to rubber after seeing people in Haiti playing with rubber balls. But rubber did not become commercialized until 1823 when Charles Macintosh, a Scottish chemist, used it to produce waterproof cloth, from which he made, among other things, waist-high fishing trousers held up with suspenders. Then in 1839 Charles Goodyear discovered the vulcanization process, which led to the industrialization of rubber. Galoshes, or rubber boots worn over shoes, started to be made in the 1850s, their name derived from the Roman word for the footwear worn by the Gauls. The first waterproof chest-high garment, what we today call fishing waders, also appeared in the 1850s, made by the Hodgman Rubber Company of New York.

The idea of wading into rivers to fish did not catch on immediately. Sir Humphry Davy said it was unhealthy. Thomas Tod Stoddart, author of the 1847 *The Angler's Companion to the Rivers and Lochs of Scotland*, complained that rubber boots did not hold up well in rivers. By the end of the nineteenth century, however, fishing magazines were writing about a new breed of fly fishers who got into the river to go after the fish.

In the 1930s lighter and more durable waterproof materials appeared. In 1931 DuPont developed a synthetic rubber called Duprene, today known as neoprene, which is not only lighter and stronger than rubber, but insulates against cold. It was not until the 1970s, however, that warmer, lighter, sturdier neoprene waders were manufactured, making it safer and more comfortable to wade into a wide cold river. By the beginning of the twenty-first century, 1.4 million waders were sold in the United States every year. Wading is now a standard way to fish.

GETTING BETTER ACCESS to fish in a river is one reason for wading, but in truth, what most fishers enjoy most about it is the experience of standing in the river, observing the flow of its riffling surface, the downstream force of its water, the sounds all around so much closer and more immediate. When you are standing in a river fishing, you feel as though you are participating in the river's life. You are, at least for a time, a river creature. Haig-Brown wrote, "Wading, one is more a part of the stream than any other way." Joan Wulff said that wading "makes me feel more closely related to the creatures within it, the fish I seek to catch."

Good, we are all agreed on that part. But we might all be making a mistake. Most fish, certainly salmon and trout, can see us. They can smell us when we are in their vicinity and they can hear our voices and footsteps. So instead of making fishing easier, wading might be scaring fish away.

An early believer in the sensory perceptions of fish was Karl von Frisch, an Austrian scientist celebrated for his work with bees. But before studying bees, Frisch studied fish. Influenced by the studies on conditioning by the Russian scientist Ivan

Pavlov, a Nobel Prize laureate in 1904, Frisch conducted those same studies with fish. He showed that if fish were always fed at the ringing of a bell, they would arrive to be fed whenever the bell rang. But Frisch's work was ridiculed—everybody knew that fish couldn't hear—so much so that he decided to stay away from fish and studied bees instead, for which work he was awarded a Nobel Prize in 1973.

Others long before Frisch's time also believed that fish could hear. Pliny, the first-century Roman naturalist, insisted that mullets could hear so well that they would come if their name was called. This presupposes they were capable of learning a name, which may be taking things too far. Aristotle thought fish could hear. So did Isaak Walton. In eighteenth-century Sweden, people were prohibited from ringing bells during fish-spawning season fearing the noise would upset the fish.

Many have also long known that fish, especially salmon, can smell. Walton was aware of this. So were Native Americans. If they were spear-fishing and a struggling fish bled in the river, fishing would be done there for a few days, they said. They also believed that when a dog came to the edge of a river, the fish could smell it and would avoid the area. Fish could smell humans on tackle, too, and many boiled their nets, traps, and wooden halibut hooks in water infused with spruce root to cover up the human scent.

And there is no doubt that fish have good vision. If they didn't, fly fishing wouldn't work. But just as the fish can see flies, so they can see fly fishers.

In old illustrations of fly fishing, the fisher is often shown crouching low in the grass or hiding behind a rock or a tree. I think of this when I fish a favorite river of mine, the Silver Creek, south of Ketchum, Idaho, with mostly bare banks and extremely clear water. I can see the trout resting in the water and they can certainly see me and probably my rod, too. I have to crouch low, step back a distance from the bank, and cast upstream so that when a fish sees my fly drifting past it will not connect the fly with me. This stealthy kind of competition is fly fishing at its most fun.

Ray Bergman, considered infallible by generations of fishers in the Northeast, cautions anglers not to "cause too much disturbance with their feet when wading." Loud splashes and sudden movements will alert the fish. So, make your way carefully through the current, try not to slip on the rocks, set your feet in a secure spot, wait a few minutes, and then cast. Rules are never infallible in fly fishing, though. One time, and only

Silver Creek, Idaho, home of smart rainbow trout

one time, I stepped into the Big Wood and immediately caught a rainbow trout. Maybe I had stepped into the river so quickly that I caught her by surprise.

A fish sees very clearly when underwater. Above water, it depends on the conditions. A bright surface may appear like a mirror to a fish. An overcast sky may make it easier for a fish to see, and choppy water definitely makes it more difficult. A trout may see big size-eleven boots and floppy waders lurching toward it more easily than it spots an angler on the bank, especially if the angler is low on the bank. As Bergman suggests, too, a wading fisher probably need not take as much care with the part of his or her body that is above water as with

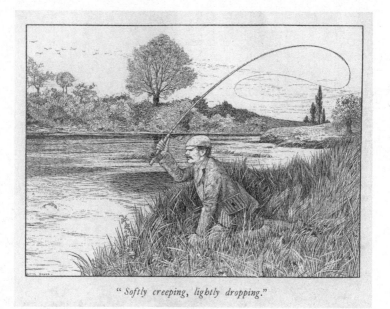

"*Softly creeping, lightly dropping.*"

Louis Rhead (American, 1857–1926), Softly creeping, lightly dropping the part that is submerged. The fish won't see your head and arms as clearly as it will see the parts stumbling underwater.

Bergman also advises fishing from the shore, keeping low to the ground, and avoiding standing with the sun behind you because silhouettes are frightening to fish. Select "backgrounds that absorb your figure," he said. All excellent advice but, since waders have been invented, most of us, most of the time, will not heed it. We like wading into the river.

Some rivers do not allow wading, however, and some guides are against it. Keith Cromae, a long-time gillie on the River Dee in Scotland, said that he wished waist-high waders were banned because they were disturbing the river.

There is considerable debate about the role of sunlight in a fish's perception of the world. In nineteenth-century Norway, salmon were said to fear shadows, even that of a bird flying overhead or the shadow of a mountain. Some old-time Norwegians also believe that salmon can predict storms and will swim fast to outrun them even before they arrive.

In many places, it is believed that fish are drawn to sunlight and feed best when the day is bright. Sunlight does silhouette the fly, which may make it more mysterious and attractive. Bergman recommended bright days. So did Humphry Davy, but he thought that when the sun is behind the fisher, casting his or her shadow onto the water, it frightens the fish. He therefore cautioned that the fisher must always stand facing the sun.

Personally, I think that it is more likely to get a bite in shade or shadows than it is in bright sunlight. This unscientific assessment is based on my own experience. I have consistently caught more fish in the shady parts of rivers than in the sunny parts, and I have definitely had better fishing days when the weather has been overcast. I was fishing the River Thurso in Sutherland, high in the northern reaches of the Scottish Highlands, on what must have been the only bright sunny day they had had in weeks. Not a bite or a nibble, but then the sun went behind a cloud and a salmon grabbed my fly. After I landed it, the sun came out again and I never saw another fish that day.

Black gnat fly

11

Fisherwomen

Beneath, a shoal of silver fishes glide,
And plays about the gilded barge's sides;
The ladies, angling in a chrystal lake,
Feast on the waters with the prey they take;
At once victorious with their lines and eyes,
They make the fishes and the men their prize.

—EDMUND WALLER (1606–87), "LADIES ANGLING"

In the long-standing mythology of fishermen there is a theory of why it is not good to fish with women and one about why it is, and both seem to be rooted in sexism.

For centuries, fishermen have claimed that women bring bad luck and poor catches. In *Holinshed's Chronicles of England, Scotland and Ireland*, a collaborative work published in 1577, an author writes that "If a woman wade through the one fresh river in the Lewis there shall no salmon be seen there for a twelve month thereafter." Of course, there is no evidence of this, and it is not clear why a sixteenth-century woman with no waterproof gear available would be wading through the freezing waters of the northern Hebrides in the first place.

I suppose a more realistic myth comes from southern Ireland. As this story goes, if you should encounter a woman (or a magpie) on your walk to the river, the fishing will not be good—a lesser cost for a more likely occurrence than the one described in *Holinshed's Chronicles*.

Many fishermen, especially fly fishermen, believe just the opposite: that women attract fish. There is no evidence or reason to support this myth either, but it is a persistent belief, and in this age of wading, I have met many fly fishermen who seriously believe that they catch more fish if there is at least one woman in the river.

Today, there are more women fly fishing than ever before, a trend that has been building slowly over centuries. Cleopatra fished in ancient Egypt or was that just a myth to make her seem more exotic and intriguing? and there were enough women fly fishers in turbulent seventeenth-century England for Edmund Waller to write the above poem about them.

Before modern times, the fly fishing world did little to accommodate women. The rods and tackle described in the *Treatyse* are very heavy; imagine trying to cast with them while wearing the long, elaborate, multilayered clothing of fifteenth-century women. Even centuries later, when a substantial number of women joined men in fly fishing, the two-handed wooden rod and heavy brass reel were not well suited for a trussed-up lady in a floor-length skirt. Nonetheless, women of that era did fly fish and caught record-size trout and salmon.

Some of the earliest records of women fly fishing come from the nineteenth-century Norwegian descriptions of the British aristocrats who set up fishing camps along their salmon rivers.

These descriptions seem to indicate that British women, at least of the upper classes, had already been doing considerable fly fishing in England. The accounts do not describe the women as novices.

In 1863 Percival Hambro and Augustus Stewart fished the Stjørdal with their wives, who were possibly the first women to fly fish a Norwegian river. The well-dressed ladies stood on the birch- and elder-covered slopes of the banks, casting into glassy pools by the rapids and falls of the rushing river, catching trophy salmon. Nineteenth-century British anglers usually

William Henry Jackson (American, 1843–1942), Fisherwoman on the Rio Grande River at Wagon Wheel Gap, *nineteenth century*

fished from banks, unless the river was too wide. Then they would fish from boats, women in long dresses among them.

Women were observed engaged in other types of fishing far earlier than they were observed fly fishing, and in Britain and America, their skill usually took men by surprise. In 1737 William Penn's daughter wrote to her brother in England saying that fishing was "her chief amusement" and asking if he could buy her "a four jointed strong fishing rod and reel and strong good line and assortment of hooks, the best sort." Since she made no mention of flies, she was probably fishing with bait.

Seventeenth- and eighteenth-century English literature occasionally makes reference to woman fishers on the estates. But it is difficult to say how many there were because no one paid much attention to them.

Theodore Gordon, the great pioneer of American fly fishing, is known to have fished with a woman, but while we know everything about his fishing, we know nothing about the woman. She was seen fishing with him in 1895, wading into a river dressed in a long skirt and leggings. Gordon sounded heartbroken, albeit unsentimental, when she left him, writing, "The best chum I ever had in fishing was a girl and she tramped just as hard and fished quite as patiently as any man I ever knew."

The state of Oregon started requiring men to purchase fishing licenses in 1899, but women were not required to have them until 1923. Some U.S. states did not require women to get fishing licenses until the 1960s.

Until recent times there were also virtually no fishing clubs for women. Andrew Burnaby in his 1798 edition of *Travels Through North America* came across a society known as "the Fishing Club," composed of sixteen women who met twice a month at the Schuylkill Club, but they were probably relegated to a room in the back. The first bona fide fishing club for women, "the Woman Fly Fishers Club," was founded in New York in 1932.

One of the great British fly fishing legends is Georgina Ballantine. On October 7, 1922, she was fishing the River Tay in Scotland on a boat handled by her father, who was the fishing official on the Glendelvine Estate through which the river runs. She was having a respectable day catching good-size salmon of twenty-five, twenty-one, and seventeen pounds. She was fishing two rods—one with a Wilkinson fly, a salmon fly with a long feathery tail, and the other with bait. A salmon grabbed the bait and she fought it for most of an hour, trying to get to the bank. The fish was so large and so strong that even when she finally got it to the bank, she could barely lift it. According to one account, she sat on it. It weighed sixty-four pounds and was four feet six inches long. That is the standing record for the largest rod-caught salmon in Britain.

But since Ballantine caught the salmon with bait, the record for catching the largest salmon with a fly was still open to challenge, and two years later, another woman, Clementina Morison, established that record. Popularly known as "Tiny" Morison, she caught a sixty-one-pound salmon on the Deveron in the Highlands with a fly known as the "Brown Wing Killer."

FOR DECADES, MARY Orvis Marbury, born in 1856, was the world's leading fly expert. Even today there are few people with the depth of knowledge she had. The daughter of Charles Orvis, she grew up during the years when her father was just starting to establish his famous fly fishing shop in Manchester, Vermont. He hired experts to teach his daughter how to tie

flies, and at the age of twenty she became head of the company's fly division. Working with her in an upstairs workshop were six other women fly-tiers. Flies were then and are still today often tied by women.

Mary Orvis established the company's mail-order catalog, which offered 434 different fly patterns. She and the other women tiers produced huge quantities of flies and tried to accommodate the wishes of as many customers as they could. If a customer described a fly that did not yet have a standardized name, Mary would find it, or tie it and name it. Many of the fly names commonly used today are hers. At one point, her father wrote to fly fishers throughout the country asking them about their favorite flies and when about two hundred wrote back, Mary added their suggestions to the company's fly selection. In 1892 she published *Favorite Flies and Their Histories*, a five-hundred-page book complete with thirty-two color plates and 290 fly patterns and their histories. It was the most complete encyclopedia of flies ever published at the time and is still a valuable resource more than a century later.

Other women set up other fly-tying shops staffed with women tiers. In 1890 Carrie Frost started up a fly-tying shop in Stevens Point, Wisconsin, and sixty years later, the town was known as America's leading fly-tying center, still staffed mostly by women.

Cornelia Crosby, often referred to as Cornelia "Fly Rod" Crosby, is a nineteenth-century Maine legend whose skill with a fly rod was only one of her outdoor talents. She was also the last hunter to legally take down a caribou in Maine. Born in 1854 in Phillips, Maine, a railroad center on the Sandy River in the interior of the state, she is said to have honed her fly fishing skills as a teenager with the help of local guides. She earned a reputation for the many large salmon and trout that she landed, and she was also known as a highly skilled fly-tier. She became a national fishing celebrity, in part because of her magazine articles, which were often about girl and women fly fishers. Railroads hired her to give talks on fly fishing destinations.

In the 1920s, when Maine was a leading fly fishing destination, one of its celebrated anglers was Carrie Stevens. In 1924, at the age of forty-two, she tied her own fly for the first time in her life. She used gray feathers, designed the fly to resemble a minnow, and—landed a thirteen-inch brook trout, a monster brook trout, only a pound smaller than the world record caught in Canada in 1915 and the largest brookie to be landed in the upper dam pool of Maine's Lake Mooselookmeguntic in thirteen years. Stevens called her fly the grey ghost, and once word of her monster trout got out, she could not tie enough of them to keep up with demand. She produced about two thousand flies a year and sold them for $1.50 each, which in today's dollars would be an annual income of fifty thousand dollars. A fly-tier has to tie a lot of flies to earn a good living.

The grey ghost, which is a streamer fly, or a fly that imitates small fish, was a pioneer. Stevens revolutionized streamers, hers being longer and narrower with the wings closer to the body than those that had come before. The grey ghost changed the way streamers were tied, and celebrity fishermen, including President Hoover and author Zane Grey, wrote or traveled to Maine to get their grey ghosts from Carrie in person.

JOAN SALVATO WULFF is one of the most respected fly fishers of modern times. She was married to noted fly fishing authority, author, and filmmaker Lee Wulff, who died in 1991, and it is a point of some frustration to her that it is usually assumed that she learned fishing from Lee. Actually, she started fishing as a child, long before she met Lee. As a five-year-old, she would go out on a boat fishing with her parents. Her father would fish and her mother would row, and it was evident to Joan that her father was having more fun than her mother. She grew up dancing and applying what she learned of rhythm and physical grace through dancing to fly-casting. It was her dream to earn her living fly fishing. How could that be done? She would have to work as a guide and teacher. Men could do that easily enough, but as a woman, she had to first convince men that she really knew how to fly fish. The means to that end was competitive fishing—women's casting competitions. Between 1943 and 1951 Joan won one or more casting competitions every year, becoming a world-champion caster. In 1951 she even won an all-male distance competition in addition to four women's titles. Now she was a recognized fly fishing champion and could finally go back to the river and make a living guiding other fishers and catching fish.

Joan has always believed that women are better suited for fly fishing than men. To her, fly fishing is the women's form of fishing because it "encompasses beauty and grace to a greater degree than any other form of fishing."

In the twentieth century, tackle more suitable for women began to be developed, starting with lightweight one-handed rods and lightweight reels. But waders presented a problem. They were not made for women, especially small women like Joan. Standing in a strong current in large, heavy, awkward waders can be dangerous. The fisher can be swept away. And there is a huge difference between standing in a river when you are over six feet tall, as Lee was, and when you are barely five feet tall, as Joan is. Joan wrote, "You know you are in trouble when you can feel the sand or pebbles running out from beneath your boots and your heels rise no matter how hard you try to get them back down." I am a fairly large man and have experienced this only once, in the Suðurland in Iceland, a fast-running river with a very sandy bottom. But for smaller people, this can be a serious problem. Joan Wulff tells women, "Don't think you can cross the same rough water a male companion can cross because he thinks you can."

Waders more suitable for women started to be introduced in the mid-1970s. Joan Wulff credits the 1978 Uniroyal Red Ball Division with "revolutionizing" fly fishing with their

LIFE *magazine, 1946*

"fly-weight" waders, chest-high garments made of polyurethane-coated nylon that weighed only three ounces. She claimed that she could dance in them. A slightly heavier version of these waders, made so they would last longer, was later developed.

Today, about 6.5 million Americans fly fish. A third of them are women, and that percentage is growing. People in the sport-fishing industry like to say that women are the fastest-growing demographic group in fly fishing, but in fact they are the only demographic group that is showing significant growth. In 2016 more than two million women were fly fishing, an increase of 142,000 over 2015. The leading outfitters, including Orvis, have launched education and training programs to bring more women into the sport. Soon fly fishing will no longer be a male bastion.

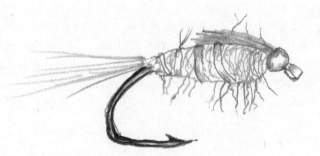

Gold-ribbed hare's ear nymph fly

12

Difficult Thoughts

*My triumphant joy abruptly faded, giving way to wonder at
the cold detachment I felt toward my prey. The fish seemed to
be observing me, too, with a sense of cold detachment as it faced
the cold detachment of a fisherman's power over life and death.
Time slipped away in our mutual gaze. Then the fish died.*

—Bei Dao, *City Gate, Open Up*

While today most fishers refer to "catching" fish, the
common phrase used to be "killing" fish. A fisherman
might say, "I killed a lot of trout today." And "killer" is often
part of the name of a fly pattern. Tiny Morison's Brown Wing
Killer is famous; another popular fly is known as "the
annihilator."

You could say that a good fly kills. But in reality, the fly
only captures and the fisher decides whether or not to kill.

In earlier centuries considerable quantities of fish were killed.
In 1854 Llewelyn Lloyd asked friends to send fishing recollec-
tions from Norway. One Mr. C. wrote: "I find by my fishing

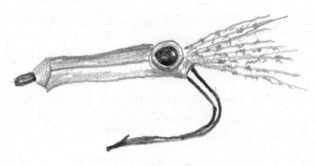

Annihilator fly

book, that in 1842 I killed in the Namsen three hundred and twenty three fish . . . from 15th of June to 8th of August." There were many similar accounts. Kill, not catch, was the stated goal.

But as decades passed and fish became more scarce, some anglers began to struggle with this. This was, of course, only a dilemma for sports fishermen. For other fishers, the whole purpose of fishing was to kill for food. Native Americans, who have never been comfortable with the concept of sports fishing, find fly fishing particularly distasteful, since it seems to be about tormenting fish for the fun of it.

Adrian Latimer, a writer with the North Atlantic Salmon Fund, which opposes commercial Atlantic salmon fishing but does not oppose fly fishing, posed this question for thought on fly fishing for salmon: "Should we really be fishing for creatures that have to struggle so hard to live?" Among fly fishers this is not a new question. Two centuries ago, Humphry Davy wrote, "All these enjoyments might be obtained without the necessity of torturing and destroying an unfortunate animal, that the true lover of nature would wish to see happy in a true scene of loveliness." Sportsmen often reject this point of view as totally unrealistic and point out that Davy also said, "I have already admitted the danger of analyzing too closely, the moral character of any of our field sports."

Many fly fishers today catch and release their fish. Indeed, many rivers require it. Europeans tend to talk about this approach as if it were new and progressive, but there is nothing new about it. Some fishers, troubled by the idea of killing fish they weren't planning to eat, have done the same for centuries. Personally, I have always released most of the fish I catch, as have many others. Growing up in New England, I used to see neighbors coming home with unseemly quantities of bluefish, which they desperately tried to give away. Some solved the problem by buying smoking machines, which allowed them to put up huge quantities of smoked bluefish to eat later. But I always thought a better solution would be to unhook the fish and put them back in the river while they were still alive. Fishers don't like to unhook bluefish because they can hurt your fingers with their sharp teeth—but what's the problem with unhooking a trout or a salmon?

Catch-and-release fishing became popular, at least in the United States, more than fifty years ago as a conservation measure. In the 1940s Lee Wulff started promoting the idea that the pleasure of salmon fly fishing lay in luring the fish, playing it on the line, and landing it, and that once that goal had been achieved, the fish should carefully be released. His famous line was, "A good game fish is too valuable to be caught only once." Haig-Brown was another early promoter of catch-and-release.

Many fly fishers find catch-and-release a convenient way to absolve them of guilt. But, if the pun can be forgiven, it does not really get them off the hook. The Native Americans may be right: fly fishers may be tormenting the fish they don't want and then throwing them back in a manner that is tremendously disrespectful to the fish.

Given the current popularity of fly fishing, catch-and-release has become an absolute necessity. Rivers like the Big Wood in Idaho or the Battenkill in Vermont could not survive the onslaught of summer anglers if the fish were not released back into the waters.

There is some debate about how much pain a fish feels. Humphry Davy, who was a great chemist but not a biologist, dismissed the idea altogether: "I think it is not to be doubted that the nervous system of fish, and cold-blooded animals in general, is less sensitive than that of warm-blooded animals."

Others have been more concerned about the pain of the bait than the pain of the target fish (an argument for fly fishing, which does not use live bait). In an 1836 book, *An Angler's Rambles*, writer Edward Jesse suggests that the angler's cruelty toward trout is nothing compared to his or her cruelty toward worms. Similarly, J. Harrington Keane in his 1887 *Fly Fishing and Fly-Making* argues against using small fish for bait, stating, "that fish feel exquisite pain on the wounding of their bodies, I cannot doubt. The barbarous method of bass and other fishing that compels the passing of a hook under the skin of a minnow, shows by the shudder and quivers of agony in the luckless bait how fearfully it suffers." He doesn't even mention that the hapless creature is being fed to a larger fish, however, or discuss the pain that the hook of an artificial fly may cause a trout or salmon.

Some fishers do not believe that hooks caught in the cartilage of a fish's mouth cause pain. Joan Wulff argues that if it were painful, fish would not pull so hard against it; some pull so hard they tear up their mouths.

Theodore Gordon, the father of dry-fly fishing, thought that the pain of the hook was only a small part of the trauma that a fly fisher, and especially a dry-fly fisher, caused a fish. He also believed that fish fight because they are terrified:

> I fancy that the dry fly frightens the fish more than the wet fly. Our friend the trout has just taken several tasty natural flies and sees another sailing down upon his nose. He rises with the greatest confidence, and the supposed insect grabs him ferociously, nearly pulls his head off and sticks a needle in his jaw. No wonder he goes wild with fright and races all over the river.

The more you fish, the more you are forced to confront these issues. Some anglers give up fishing because they cannot make their peace with them, but most find a way to do so, largely because they want to keep fishing. Here is Zane Grey's reasoning:

> As a man, and a writer who is forever learning, fishing is still a passion, stronger with all the years, but tempered by an understanding of the nature of primitive man, hidden in all of us, and by a keen reluctance to deal pain to any creature. The sea and the river and the mountain have almost taught me not to kill except for the urgent needs of life; and the time will come when I shall have grown up to that. When I read a naturalist or a biologist I am always ashamed of what I have called a sport. Yet one of the truths of evolution is that not to practice strife, not to use violence, not to fish or hunt—that is to say, not to

fight—is to retrograde as a natural man. Spiritual and intellectual growth is attained at the expense of the physical.

Fishing is something that we feel the need to do, even though, as Grey puts it, "the fish are incidental." Humans are more complicated than fish. Fish may understand our urge to catch them, but they would not understand our reservations about doing so even if we could somehow communicate our thoughts to them. Quickly it is argued that with fish it is a means of survival but for us it is an entertainment, but that is not always the case either. A salmon in a river does not eat and yet chases flies. This too may be for the sport of it.

The claim is continually made that catch-and-release does not work because the released fish does not survive. To any experienced fly fisher this is clearly not true. Don't be fooled, it is said, because the released fish appears to be merrily swimming home. It will die later. But in a catch-and-release fishery, it is common to catch a fish that shows scars of previous hooks or even marks of lines. Poet Elizabeth Bishop once described such a veteran fish in "The Fish":

> and then I saw
> that from his lower lip
> —if you could call it a lip—
> grim, wet, and weaponlike,
> hung five old pieces of fish-line,
> or four and a wire leader
> with the swivel still attached,
> with all their five big hooks

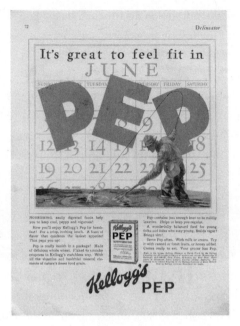

1927 ad for Pep cereal

grown firmly in his mouth.
A green line, frayed at the end
where he broke it, two heavier lines,
and a fine black thread
still crimped from the strain and snap
when it broke and he got away.
Like medals with their ribbons
frayed and wavering,
a five-haired beard of wisdom
trailing from his aching jaw.

A few may not survive and many are caught numerous times.
With each experience they grow wiser. Salmonids are capable

of learning. Haig-Brown examined numerous studies on this subject. The goal of the fisherman is to play the fish until it is completely exhausted. Only then will it allow itself to be landed. When a fish is in such a state, it has a high concentration of lactic acid in its blood. Too high a concentration results in the death of a fish. Mammals can undergo the same process. In mammals, once the stress stops, the lactic acid abates. With fish the lactic acid can continue building for several hours. So a caught fish can be released and appear to swim away in good health and then die several hours later. The studies that Haig-Brown examined concluded that this happens in 20 percent or fewer cases, so most fish released in fresh water survive.

An idea that has been gaining in popularity in recent years is to use hooks without barbs. The barb is a sharp point on the hook that is pointed in the opposite direction of the hook. If a fish tries to flip off a hook, it is only trapped even more securely on the barb. No matter which way the fish turns, the hook is embedded more deeply.

Originally, hooks made of bone or ivory or shell had no barb, though a few Native American bone hooks of a later period did. Egyptians started making copper hooks about 3100 B.C., but they, too, did not have barbs. Not until about 1878 B.C., during the rule of Egypt's Twelfth Dynasty, did hooks start to be made with barbs. In time the Egyptians also learned to taper those barbs so that their holes would stay small and be harder to wriggle out of. Roman hooks were barbed and sometimes double barbed.

Until recently, barbless hooks were used only in hatcheries, where extra care is taken not to harm the fish. And that is the point. A fish can be released in far better condition when caught with a barbless hook. But a barbless hook greatly reduces a fisher's chance of landing a fish—a challenge that is in keeping with the entire idea of fly fishing, which is all about making fishing difficult.

I find the concept of using barbless hooks appealing, but I would only use them in certain places. On European rivers where it seems an absolute miracle to hook an Atlantic salmon and keep it on the hook even with a barb, I think I want to stick with a barb. This means that extra care needs to be taken in unhooking the fish. But if using a barbless hook means catching only three rainbows instead of six on a western river or only thirty fish instead of the sixty-five I once caught in a few days on the Ozernaya River in Russia, I think I would enjoy the challenge of it. On the Wood River in Idaho I have long used barbless hooks because they are required. On a heavily fished catch-and-release river such as the Wood, it is important that the fish are released in good condition.

Even a fish caught on a barbless hook can be harmed by bad handling—by being squeezed too hard or grabbed by the gills, for example. Most other types of fishers don't worry too much about such issues, but those who choose to fly fish are the kind of people prone to ponder.

President Jimmy Carter offered the hard truth when he wrote, "Those of us who habitually release trout know that on occasion even a barbless hook will kill." Carter advised that there was no way to completely remove the role of predator from fishing and that if the fisherman could not make peace with this reality, the solution was to not fish. A few fishers reach this conclusion and give up fishing but most accept, even sometimes reluctantly, their role in nature.

Hair frog surface bug fly

13

Fishing for Words

I refuse to rise
To the tempting fly
Of the message I was sent
Feathered with bright poetry.
I am too wise a fish
To gobble the angler's bait;
These are troubled waters.
But I can avoid being caught.

—Njála Saga (pronounced NYOLA),
THIRTEENTH–CENTURY ICELANDIC SAGA ABOUT
EVENTS IN ICELAND BETWEEN 960 AND 1020

U p until a recent growth of books on all kinds of fishing,
fly fishing was the most written about form of fishing.
Books on fly fishing can be divided into two categories: books
that address the question "Why do we fish?" and books that
answer the question "How do we fish?" The first type moves

us and the second instructs us. The first are for everyone and the second, uniquely for fishers.

There are many books with advice on how to fish by authors such as Lee Wulff, Ray Bergman, and Roderick Haig-Brown. These writers have been enormously influential. Most anyone who fished the Catskills studied Bergman. Wulff, associated with Atlantic salmon more than trout, was hugely influential in popularizing dry-fly fishing and short fly rods. He also tirelessly developed and experimented with new flies for particular situations.

Some fly fishing books are more about travel than fishing, their subject being "where I have gone fishing." Novelist Thomas McGuane's fishing memoir *The Longest Silence* is a good example of this. Zane Grey, famed as an author of Western adventure novels, wrote five of the best of this genre.

Zane Grey's fictions took place in the West, but his nonfiction fishing "tales" are also set in the Gulf Stream, the Amazon, or the Everglades. He told his stories well and had thoughtful messages about humankind and nature, even though he could occasionally be shockingly colonialist, as in a photograph taken in Mexico captioned "the Author and his Indian."

According to Grey, the reason why there are so many books about fly fishing is that fly fishers are essentially egotists; he included Isaak Walton as an example. "There is some strange spell haunting stream and lake, and it persuades most anglers to have faith in experience that they think is wisdom," he wrote.

Grey was writing in the 1920s when, as in Walton's day, fly fishing was not distinguished from other kinds of fishing. Grey was a fly fisherman, a bait fisherman, and a spinning and lure fisherman, often in the same river, sometimes on the same day.

Literary Digest, *1935*

For him, choosing which fishing technique to use was like choosing which fly to use. What will work in this circumstance? What are the alternatives? When writing about the Rogue in Oregon, which he, and many others, considered one of the great rivers of the world, he noted, "Steelhead are caught in abundance with bait, salmon eggs spinners, and spoons." Today, fishers are banned from using anything but flies on whole sections of the Rogue during prime fishing season. The need for conservation has given flies the moral high ground. It is simply too easy to catch fish with these other methods—not sporting.

Yet even today I sometimes see the lines blurring. When failing to catch fish with flies in Norway, my Norwegian friends unabashedly turned to spinning tackle and live bait. I also found locals on the Eyak River in Alaska fishing for sockeye with salmon eggs attached to their flies. And I encountered the same technique being used for catching king salmon in the Willamette in Oregon.

FOR SOME REASON, when it comes to creative writing on fly fishing, there seems to be far more poetry than fiction. To begin with, both Isaak Walton and Charles Cotton considered themselves to be poets first and foremost. Gervase Markham, Thomas Barker, and many other early fly fish writers were also poets. In England, Scotland, and Ireland, writing poetry and fly fishing seemed to go hand in hand. William Butler Yeats, Robert Burns, John Donne, Ted Hughes—all wrote poems about fly fishing, as did a few New Englanders such as Robert Lowell. Fly fishing, it seems, is a poetic subject.

Short stories and novels on the subject are much rarer. And, it is interesting to note that most of the prose literature on fishing hovers between fiction, autobiography, and nonfiction. For writers who fish the subject is often seen as poetic enough without the devices of fiction. And a fishing trip is sometimes a great story without the need to fictionalize it. And maybe nonfiction allows more room for expressing such details as fly preferences. Why did McGuane, an accomplished novelist, choose nonfiction to write about fly fishing?

There are a few forgotten novels about fly fishing. Among the many obscure small-edition British books about salmon fishing in Norway is a novel by Mary Kennard, a popular nineteenth-century novelist whose work often had sporting themes. *Landing a Prize* is her Victorian romance about an

Englishman who goes to Norway to fish and comes home with a Norwegian bride. The romance sections of the book are a bit tedious, but the fishing descriptions are excellent.

Many nonfiction fishing books hang on the idea that fishing is a metaphor for the larger subject of human nature. Roderick Haig-Brown was a fishing writer of unusual grace who once said, "I am a writer first and a fisherman second. I go fishing quite a lot and think about fishing a lot, but I write all the time." An Englishman, Haig-Brown wrote fiction as well as nonfiction and both are set in British Columbia, where he lived most of his life. His novels are about a range of subjects. *Starbuck Valley Winter* is about trapping, *Saltwater Summer* is about commercial salmon fishing, and *The Whale People* is about a Native American group. Among the nearly forty short stories that he wrote are a number about fly fishing, all written in the same elegant style as his nonfiction.

Haig-Brown's daughter Valerie was convinced that all her father's stories were based on actual events and even recalled when a few of them actually took place. The fishing details in his stories reveal an author who knew a lot about fly fishing, but the heart of his stories always touches us with a broader meaning.

Haig-Brown's "The Wharf," published in the *New Yorker* in 1950, is a coming-of-age story about a boy deemed too small to ever land a thirty-pound salmon. But one day he does, only to drop it back into the water while trying to weigh it to prove that he had done it. "Black Fishermen" is one of the rare really good dog stories, perhaps comparable to Thomas Mann's "Bashan and I," which is about his German short-haired pointer. Haig-Brown's story is about a Labrador retriever, a dog bred in Labrador to jump in icy water and help a fishermen retrieve his cod. In this story a Lab loved going fly fishing and jumping in the water to help land salmon.

DESPITE THE HISTORY and lore of fly fishing as an amusement for aristocrats, few authors wrote about aristocrats fly fishing. One rare exception was Arthur Train. Starting in 1919, Train wrote stories for the *Saturday Evening Post*, later anthologized in a book published by Scribner's, about a tough, fair-minded, and incredibly sly defense attorney named Ephraim Tutt. He hailed from Pottsville, a mythical town in New York's Mohawk Valley where life was simple and the fishing was good.

In Train's 1933 "Mr. Tutt Is No Gentlemen," the legal crowd from Pottsville travels to their exclusive fly fishing club on Canada's Cascapédia River. The elite have always been drawn to this river because it is both a great fishing river and difficult and expensive to get to; it is that old and disturbing idea that fly fishermen belong to a fraternity. In the story, the Pottsville elite is competing for a trophy for the largest salmon. A judge who is a stickler for the written law but not the unwritten law of fishermen is among the group. He determines that under the written law, a salmon belongs not to the person who hooks it but to the person who lands it, supporting Walton's claim that you can't lose a fish because it was never yours. The judge says that if someone has a salmon on their line and someone else reaches over with a gaff, a landing pole, and lands it, the fish belongs to the one who gaffed it. Obviously, this is not an acceptable way for a fisherman to behave even though it may be legal. The judge hooks into a prize fish that Tutt is trying to land and gets it away from him. The rest of the story is about how Tutt tricks the judge out of the salmon, thereby preserving the code of fishermen, not the law.

RICHARD BRAUTIGAN'S *Trout Fishing in America* is an example of a fishing book that is not specifically about fishing. Written in 1962 and published in 1967, the Delta paperback, with an untitled cover showing Brautigan and his first wife, Virginia Alder, in San Francisco, resembles the iconic counterculture record covers of the 1960s. On the back is a quote attributed to the Viking Press: "Mr. Brautigan submitted a book to us in 1962 called *Trout Fishing in America*. I gather from the reports that it was not about trout fishing."

Though this quote is a perfect counterculture way to frame the book, it is not exactly true. It is evident from the book that Brautigan was a member of the fishing fraternity. He knew a great deal about fly fishing and his book offers excellent descriptions of good rivers and how to fish them. He even gives a solid bibliography of historic fly fishing books, though in a very Brautigan way. For example, he tells a story of catching a trout and giving it a sip of port wine, which kills it, and then lists the many important books on fly fishing that failed to note that port would kill a fish. Oddly he doesn't include mention of Isaak Walton's famous book in this list. He makes up for this later, toward the end of the book, when he suggests a placard for the ban-the-bomb movement that reads: "Isaak Walton Would've Hated the Bomb!"

In American letters and culture, Brautigan marks the transition from beatnik to hippie (though he always claimed to

The original Delta paperback cover for Trout Fishing in America *shows Brautigan and his wife, Virginia Alder, but no title or author name*

dislike hippies). Raised in poverty in the Pacific Northwest, he made his way to San Francisco in the 1950s and was a beat poet. He then became interested in prose, but his short meandering "novels" with their strong sense of rhythm, little plot, beautiful language, and whacky sense of humor still seem a bit like beat poetry.

In 1961 Brautigan received a $350 tax refund, with which he bought a ten-year-old Plymouth station wagon, and with a Coleman stove, tent, Royal typewriter, crate of books, and fishing tackle (not deluxe, but not junk either: he had a seven-foot-long, two-piece RA Special #240 bamboo fly rod and an

Olympus reel), drove off to camp in Idaho with his wife and their daughter, Ianthe. This was the basis of his "novel" *Trout Fishing in America.*

Perhaps I relate to this book a little more than some because I have fished a number of the same rivers Brautigan fished—the Big Wood, Silver Creek, Salmon, and Snake. Fly fishers will not always find his insights useful. Sometimes it is standard, "I fished Graveyard Creek in the dusk when the hatch was on and worked some good trout out there." It is "working" the trout, not necessarily catching them, that matters. And the setting is everything. At other times, the book is mystifying, as when it observes, "Trout fishing is one of the best things in the world for remembering children's names." Or, "I remember mistaking an old woman for a trout stream in Vermont. I had to beg her pardon."

Brautigan writes of going to a San Francisco junkyard to "buy" a used trout stream, and through this seemingly absurd anecdote lays out the true requirements for a great stream: clear water, trees, flowers, animals, and insects. He satirizes fly fashions with his story describing the lengthy process by which Leonardo da Vinci designed the "Last Supper" lure.

The fact that Brautigan took most of his material from real life does not mean his book is grounded in reality. He turns a legless street person whom he knew in San Francisco into "Trout Fishing in America Shorty" and throughout the book tries to ship him to Chicago author Nelson Algren, who he is convinced would like him as a character.

Though Brautigan was a genuine fly fisherman, it has been suggested that his use of fishing as background material was an attempt to emulate his literary hero, Ernest Hemingway. He was in Idaho when Hemingway killed himself in nearby

Ketchum (as was I), an occurrence that shook him greatly and is mentioned in the book. Sadly, too, the influence of Hemingway on Brautigan may have been at play in 1984 when he ended his own life by firing a .44 Magnum into his head.

Trout Fishing in America was hailed by critics as a masterly work that gave birth to "the post-modern novel," and the book turned the unknown marginal Brautigan into an international star. He never had another great success, however. For fly fishers, perhaps his greatest contribution to the sport was his dispelling of the notion that fly fishing is for the elite. Seeing this offbeat vagabond, living on the fringes, casting into a river pool whenever he found one, did much to change the image of fly fishing.

WHEN THINKING OF fly fishing fiction, most people probably think of Ernest Hemingway, but although he did a great deal of fly fishing, he did not write much about it. Fly fishing appears in only two of his works—a two-part short story titled "Big Two-Hearted River" and the novel *The Sun Also Rises*. It is significant that both of these are early works written in the 1920s. Hemingway apparently lost interest in fly fishing later in life, especially after he started hooking giant marlin in the Gulf Stream.

Hemingway was taught to fly fish by his father when he was very young and did it most of his life. He was never the dedicated expert his son Jack became, but fished often with wet flies, not dry ones like Jack. He usually fished a McGinty on top with two other wetflies lower on the line, which are known as "drops." For a famously decisive man this was a very indecisive way to fish, the theory being that with three flies in the water—difficult to cast, by the way—something is bound to work.

But he was still probably more of a fly fisherman than most of his characters. When he started fishing in the northern Rockies in the 1930s there were no tackle shops and he ordered everything from a famous British catalog, *Angler's Guide and Catalogue* by the Hardy Brothers in England. He fished exclusively with Hardy Brothers tackle until he was in his fifties and the trunk with all his tackle disappeared. Then he stopped fly fishing. He was living in Cuba and pursuing big-game fish by then.

In "Big Two-Hearted River," Nick Adams has returned weary from war and restores, almost cleanses, himself by going fishing for trout in his favorite river in the Upper Peninsula of Michigan. Many of Hemingway's early stories were inspired by the trauma he suffered from being wounded by a trench mortar on the Italian Front in World War I. Only a fisher could understand the idea of treating psychological problems by going fishing. He writes that his character was able "to leave everything behind" including "the need for thinking." This is the true fishing experience. When Hemingway came home from World War One, his leg shattered and suffering from nightmares and cold sweats, he returned in 1919 to the Fox River, in the Upper Peninsula, where he had fished in his childhood. These stories are Hemingway at his most beautiful as they simply and gracefully describe the great curative powers of fly fishing. I am surprised that everybody didn't take up fly fishing after this story was published.

Originally, when he wrote the story in 1924, it was about a great deal more than fishing. It was the longest story he had ever written and he broke it into parts one and two. It was one of the first works to show the power of Hemingway writing. It included long pages of autobiographical reminiscences on early fishing days and even contemporaries in Paris. At the urging of friends, including Gertrude Stein and Ezra Pound, he cut so that it was just this veteran going fishing. Even the character's traumatic war experiences are only vaguely alluded to so that the reader senses it but is not given it—it is just about fishing and trying to clear his mind. It was one of the origins of what became famous as Hemingway's "iceberg theory" of writing, that much is not explained and is hidden underneath for the reader to sense.

But there are a couple of factual problems in the story, if one considers facts to be relevant to fiction. Nick Adams is literally, but not technically, fly fishing. He gathers grasshoppers, puts them in a jar that he ties around his neck, and takes them out one by one to put on a hook. There is a legitimate fly that resembles a grasshopper, but a real grasshopper is bait and bait fishing is not allowed on the fly-only Upper Michigan rivers.

"Big Two-Hearted River" was published in 1925, when Hemingway's first-born son John, known as Jack, was two years old. When Jack was an adult and a dedicated fly fisherman, he decided to fish his father's old rivers, including the Two Hearted River. But he found that the river was not very good for fishing, and he caught little. When he complained to his father, Ernest smiled and explained that the Two Hearted had never been very good for fishing. He just loved the name.

Fly fishing plays a similar role in *The Sun Also Rises*. After a hard week with friends, getting drunk, attacking each other, and having fistfights, Bill and Jake, the only two of the group who act like friends, are supposed to restore their sanity by escaping to fish the Irati in northern Navarre, Spain. I have fished the Irati. It is wide, curvaceous, and gravel-bottomed, with smooth and riffled surfaces, the kind of river to find trout in, or to use Hemingway language, "a trouty river." The Irati mumbles its way past towns with narrow stone streets and red-roofed square Basque houses, surrounded by mountains of green velvet with dark rocky crests. It is one of the beautiful places of the earth.

But there is a disagreement between Bill and Jake. Bill wants to fly fish and Jake, who is a Hemingway-like character, wants to bait fish with worms. Jake offers Bill a few worms. He wants his friend to catch trout and the odds are better with worms. But Bill is a purist who would rather fly cast and catch nothing than fish with worms. He refuses Jake's offer, saying, "If they won't take a fly, I'll just flick it around."

Bill fishes with a McGinty fly, a charming detail because today almost no one uses them. The McGinty was invented in 1883 by Charles McGinty, who, like Hemingway, was from Chicago. With its yellow-and-black chenille body, white-tipped mallard wings, and red hackle tail, it resembles a bee that has fallen into the water. Drifting downstream, it looked tasty to trout. But it is almost a forgotten fly today.

Since McGinty flies are not available in most shops anymore, I decided to tie one of my own. But I could not find the required white-tipped brown mallard feathers for the wings. Then one day on the sidewalk outside my Manhattan apartment I found two white dove feathers, from the rock doves everyone in New York calls pigeons. I dyed part of one with a brown Sharpie. Sharpies use an alcohol-based dye that holds up well in water. Fly fishing is all about improvising, though you probably shouldn't admit you use Sharpies for your flies.

I haven't fished with my McGinty yet because I have to find a river where bees are pollinating and floating downstream. Or, according to Hemingway, travel to the Irati in July. I would love to fish the Irati again.

It is odd that in both "Big Two-Hearted River" and *The Sun also Rises*, the character who seems to be based on the author—in the original draft of *The Sun Also Rises* the Jake character was named "Hem"—favors bait fishing. Hemingway often liked to contradict his own beliefs and then stage an argument. In his hunting books hunting is denounced and argued about, despite Hemingway being a lifelong hunter. In *The Sun Also Rises* Bill and Jake are in a fly-versus-bait fishing contest and although in most such competitions bait fishers win, Bill with his McGinty holds his own—even slightly outperforms Jake with his worms. It seems that Hemingway had a deeper faith in flies than is sometimes supposed. We know from his letters that he was a fly and not bait fisherman and often, like Bill, not Jake, fished with a McGinty.

IT IS NOT an exaggeration to say that among fiction books on fly fishing, there is none better than Irishman Maurice Walsh's *Green Rushes*. When the Irish write about fly fishing, they are writing not just about a sport, but about a way of life, about Irish culture. *Green Rushes* is a series of interconnected stories about people who fought in the Black and Tan War. The most famous of the stories is "The Quiet Man," because in 1952 John Ford made it into a movie starring John Wayne and Maureen O'Hara. In the original story the man is not as big as John Wayne, which is important because his larger brother-in-law is bullying him. He is not an American either, though he was a prize fighter in America. He returns to Ireland to fight for Irish independence.

The Black and Tan War was the cruel brainstorm of Winston Churchill, who in 1920 recruited embittered out-of-work World War One combat veterans into the Royal Irish Constabulary to fight the Irish Republican Army. The British troops were called Black and Tans after the colors of their makeshift uniforms and were infamous for their vicious attacks on civilians. When their men were killed, they avenged their deaths with reprisals that included mass killings of civilians and the burning of towns. They were so hated that they pushed the IRA to fight harder than ever and earned the Irish people the sympathy of the British public. The war ended in 1922 with independence.

In the story, an elite squadron of the IRA called the Flying Column are weary of the war, tired of the killing. As they wander around southwestern Ireland, plotting attacks on the Black and Tans (assassinations, kidnappings, sabotage) and trying not to get caught, which would mean certain death, they spend a great deal of time thinking about fly fishing. They are in the counties of Cork and Shannon, through which the Blackwater and the Shannon, two of Ireland's best salmon rivers, and their tributaries flow. They examine every brook and river they pass for good pools to return to and fish later. Passing one such stream, one character reflects, "There would be fish in water like that, I consider lazily: speckled trout gourmandizing on the may-fly, or maybe, a clean run salmon up from Shannon River."

But the squadron is also in an area of the most vicious fighting of the war. The Black and Tan even burned the city of Cork. In one scene an IRA fighter named Owen is ordered on a mission by a superior named Hugh Forbes. "He was more intensely

Republican than Hugh Forbes himself, and was afraid of nothing in this world or the next," writes the narrator. And yet Owen refuses Forbes's order. "You'll have your reasons?" asks Forbes.

"I have," says Owen. "I'm going fishing."

At times the story turns dark, but even then, there is always fishing. One fighter reflects, "Only yesterday I killed clean-run salmon down there, and now, this still summer noon, I was set to kill men—or to be killed."

In one of my favorite stories in *Green Rushes*, "Then Came the Captain's Daughter," a British officer arrives at his wartime posting in Ireland with his sister and fly fishing tackle. He is a Scot and some of the Flying Column fighters had fished with him in Scotland before the war. Ignoring their state of war, they all spend time fishing together. But then one day the IRA fighters realize that they have inadvertently laid out top-secret plans that were overheard by the officer and his sister. They try to make the officer promise not to reveal what he has heard, but he says that he cannot do that.

What to do? The normal practice would be to shoot them both. But the fighters cannot shoot their fishing companions. There are rumors of a settlement and the war might soon be over. The fighters take the officer and his sister to a remote spot with excellent fishing and tell them that they are prisoners who must stay there and fish until the war is over. But, of course, they cannot be left unguarded, the fighters must take their turns fishing with them. When the war ends, Ireland is free and so are they.

THE HISTORY OF Norman Maclean's *A River Runs Through It* helps to explain why there are so few works of fiction about fly fishing. Today, this largely autobiographical novella about growing up fishing in Montana is considered one of the most beautiful of fly fishing books, required reading for anyone who owns a fly rod, far more so than Walton. But for many years Maclean, a University of Chicago English teacher, could not find a publisher for it. Finally, in 1976, the University of Chicago Press did publish it, but few people might have ever read it were it not for Robert Redford. After considerable squabbling with Maclean, he got his permission to turn the book into the film. By the time the film was released in 1992, Maclean had died.

The film captured the romance and mysticism of fly fishing as described in the novella and caused a growth in the sport's popularity. Suddenly, fly fishing became a trendy thing to do. I often wonder if the novices who took it up after seeing the film were disappointed once they realized that the extravagant rod casting of Brad Pitt, those loops and swirls back and forth over the water, are not really the way trout are caught. Fly fishing involves using smaller, more precise movements, and the only time a fisher might use large sweeping moves is when trying to dry out a fly while dry-fly fishing. False casting, or "shadow casting" as it is called in the film, is a technique that is used at times, but it involves only one or two modest sweeps before letting go of the line. Luring a trout to rise by passing the fly back and forth over the surface of the water seldom works. It usually scares away the fish.

Both the novella and the film strike deeply into questions of why we fish and what it means. And though the story is always focused on fly fishing, it is about something much more profound. It is about the relationship between Norman Maclean, a straitlaced and responsible kid and then man, and his wildly irresponsible brother, Paul. Yet Paul has a great saving grace: he is a superb fly fisherman and though the two brothers are far apart in many ways, they are always close when fly fishing. Fly fishing holds this family together.

To Maclean, his father, and his brother—there are no women fishing in this story—fly fishing was a religion. The father is a minister, but the opening lines of the book establish that "In our family there was no clear line between religion and fly fishing." Fly fishing is what you ought to be doing and you ought to be doing it well. You are a fly fisherman or nothing. Paul theorizes, "Practically everybody on the West Coast was born in the Rocky Mountains where they failed as fly fishermen, so they migrated to the West Coast and became lawyers, certified public accountants, presidents of airline companies, gamblers, or Mormon missionaries."

To the Macleans, dry-fly fishing is the highest and holiest activity; bait fishing is a sacrilege. They understand what fishing can be and how rewarding it is to get it right. Fly fishing is an escape to a better world.

If you are a fly fisher, this book expresses better than any other why you do it. If you are not a fly fisher, it explains to you what compels those who are. "I took my time walking down the trail, trying with each step to leave the world behind. Something within fishermen tries to make fishing into a world perfect and apart." There is always that moment, boots on, stepping down into the river, like slipping through a magic portal.

I HAVE TO mention Ota Pavel's *How I Came to Know Fish* because even though I have a prejudice against bait fishers, this book has a deeper understanding of recreational fishing than any other book I know. Every time I reread this small book I am surprised that its author is a bait fisherman, not a fly fisherman, for his fine sensitivity about fishing is something I associate uniquely with fly fishers.

Pavel was a Czech journalist and sports writer. He came from rural Czechoslovakia. He may have never even seen fly fishing as a child. He and his friends fished for carp, or sometimes fat chub, barbell, or pike "the size of crocodiles." They used bread or dough as bait, a folk way of fishing all over the world. In *Trout Fishing in America*, Brautigan talked about how he would take a slice of bread from breakfast and roll its soft center into balls to put on the hook. Brautigan added, "I ended up being my own trout and eating the slice of bread myself."

During Pavel's childhood, hungry times meant that bread would be baked and eaten by the family and the fish would go hungry. In better days, a little anise would be added to the dough, as it was believed that the spice would attract the fish.

Pavel wrote about how he would lie down in a boat with his rods set and hooks baited, a tin can resting on each rod, and go to sleep. If he got a bite, the can would wake him up. He wrote, "Of all the sleep a man can have, a fisherman's sleep is the sweetest. It is the greatest of luxuries—sleep and fishing." Such sleep is not possible while fly fishing, which is all about being alert.

Pavel's father was obsessed with fishing and Pavel caught the affliction from him. Pavel recalled his first fish: "The rod bent into an arch and, for the first time in my life, I felt the delicious pull of a fish." If you are made to be a fisher, once you have felt that delicious pull, you never forget it. It becomes part of your muscle memory and you crave it over and over again. And so it was with Ota Pavel.

On March 15, 1939, the Germans invaded Czechoslovakia. Pavel's mother was Christian and his father was Jewish. Life became very difficult. The father had his fish pond confiscated. "How can a Jew breed carp?" said the Germans. Then Pavel's father and two older brothers were deported to a concentration camp. Only nine-year-old Ota and his mother remained. They had nothing to eat.

Fishing became a different endeavor, a desperate attempt to get food. Pavel made a short, sturdy fishing rod—short enough to hide under his coat because he was not allowed to fish in the pond. The carp had become the exclusive property of the Nazis, who ate large feasts in the town's castle. Pavel could hear the refrain of "Lili Marlene" drifting out the castle windows. He made a study of the town's people so that he knew who the informants were and from whom he had to hide his fishing rod, and he learned the habits of the fish warden. Then he studied the carp so he could take them quickly and efficiently. He wrote:

> It took some time getting to know them. I had to learn
> to tell the difference between their bad and good moods.
> I had to learn to tell when they were hungry, when they
> were full, and when they felt like playing. I had to recog-
> nize where they were likely to swim, and where I would
> look for them in vain.

Pavel's father and two brothers survived and returned home, but Pavel never forgot those hard, desperate times. He continued to fish and always had nostalgia for his early fishing days. Like Norman Maclean, he particularly cherished that moment when he descended to the water to fish. "Most of all I remember how I walked or drove to the fish."

He never lost that love of the delicious pull on his hand. "A man can look at the sky. He can stare into the forest, but nobody really sees into a river. Only with a fishing rod can one look there."

In 1973 Pavel died at age of forty-two of a heart attack. As he lay dying, he talked of dreaming of his favorite river, cupping its water in his hands and kissing it, "as I would kiss a woman."

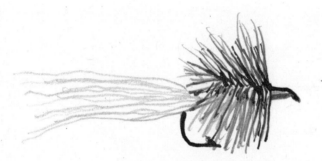

Rhodes tarpon fly

Yeats on the Blackwater

Although I can see him still—
The freckled man who goes
To a gray place on a hill
In gray Connemara clothes
At dawn to cast his flies—
It's long since I began
To call up to the eyes
This wise and simple man.

—WILLIAM BUTLER YEATS, "THE FISHERMAN"

The Blackwater is a soft-spoken burly giant of a river that makes its way insistently through green County Cork, sweeping around wide bends, snorting eagerly under old dark stone bridges. It has never offered me luck, only beauty.

Though only one hundred miles long, it is the third longest river in Ireland. It is not appropriately named. The water is not black but crystal clear, though it appears tea colored because of its brown gravel bottom. Every stone of that bottom is plainly visible. If a trout or a salmon happens by, it is visible, too.

Novelist Elizabeth Bowen, one of the great Irish novelists (I say in case it has been forgotten) and a long County Cork resident, wrote about the Blackwater in her nonfiction book about her ancestral home, *Bowen's Court*. She described the Blackwater as "most majestic and glassy," and that is exactly right. More than a century earlier, Sir Humphry Davy listed the Blackwater as one of the greatest salmon-fishing rivers in the world (his world having been England, Wales, Scotland, and Ireland).

As with most every Atlantic salmon river, there are far fewer salmon in the Blackwater today than there were in Davy's time. But it is still considered one of Ireland's two best rivers, competing only with the Moy on the Mayo–Sligo border to the northwest.

The shells of rare freshwater pearl mussels are found on the Blackwater's banks. Wild white swans live on the river, and when they fly over it in couples they sing in unison. Bright blue-backed, red-chested kingfishers, a species normally associated with the tropics, patrol the Blackwater and are capable of hovering, turning their heads to search left and right, and then diving into the water to grab small fish with their long pointed beaks. Nearby are leggy grey heron with far longer beaks that lower snaking necks to fish in the river.

White egrets grace the river's edge like fine draped linen. But they are not appreciated because they face the same distrust as newcomers do everywhere. They have only been in the Blackwater for two or three decades, which, for the Irish, who talk of conflicts from hundreds of years ago as if they happened yesterday, is a very short time. The egrets come from France,

Netting a brown trout in the Blackwater River, County Cork, Ireland

"where they belong," some locals say, and contrary to popular opinion, probably eat no more small fish than do the herons and kingfishers. They like to sit on a bank and wave their bright yellow feet, like a bold kind of salmon fly, and attract young salmon.

All these beautiful birds that I love to gaze on while I cast are bad news for the salmon fry, parr, and smolts who live and grow in the river before they are ready to take to the open sea. People find it hard to accept that this is the order of nature, and the way it is supposed to work. The birds survive because they eat the salmon eggs, and the salmon survive because they lay so many eggs that even though some are eaten, there are still plenty left to grow to full size and produce more.

Crows don't fish, but they never pass up a free meal and would eat almost anything if it were lying in front of them. They, too, are part of this river and, as is often the case with the ones that don't fish, they make the most noise. On an island in the river is a crow rookery where they sit in nests high in the trees and relentlessly shriek about the glory of the few eggs they have laid. I suppose they are right. Reproduction is worth shouting about. The trout and salmon don't seem to mind and like to swim in the deeper trenches that pass by the noisy rookery.

The land is limestone, hard limestone paths and rocky meadows and forested cliffs, interspersed with soft marshy green valleys where cattle sometimes graze. In the spring, a good time for fly fishing, wild irises bloom, and water peppermint reaches out to the river. Tall antique stone ruins stand on the hilltops. People call them castles, but they were mostly built as watchtowers.

The town that I have stayed in more than once when fishing the Blackwater is Fermoy, a small city that has little to recommend it except the river. Here, a wide stretch of the Blackwater meets the Awbeg tributary. A weir for catching salmon once obstructed the river, but fortunately the weir broke recently and the river now passes freely. Between the thirteenth and fifteenth century, a ferry crossed the Blackwater at this spot and in 1626, a bridge was built. It washed away two years later, but in 1687, Robert Boyle, the famous scientist who was from the region, built a new limestone bridge.

Fermoy is not an ancient town. It was designed by John Anderson, a Scot who had grown wealthy on commerce in the town of Cork. He bought the future site of Fermoy in 1791 and began to design the town. Seven years later, rebellion broke out and the British flooded Ireland with soldiers. Anderson offered to build barracks for them in Fermoy. He also rebuilt and enlarged Boyle's limestone bridge. Fermoy became an affluent British garrison town and remained so for decades. The bridge was enlarged again in 1865, and handsome small houses were built for the officers.

With the officers came fly fishing—the British army officers always took fly fishing with them wherever they were posted. Word of the Blackwater spread, too, and it became a popular river for English fly fishers, military and civilian. The British army left the town in 1921, but the British still go to the Blackwater to fish. In 2015 the bridge was renamed the Thomas Kent Bridge for Tomás Ceannt, a "patriot" who fought the British and was executed by them in Cork in 1916. The British are welcome to fish but the Irish are not about to forget.

I WAS FISHING with Glenda Powell, who is considered the best caster, guide, and teacher in Ireland. I had found her after asking friends in Galway to recommend a really good gillie, and everyone said, "Get more than a gillie, get Glenda and fish the Blackwater." A gillie takes a client to good fishing spots, picks the flies, and maybe ties them on, but does not necessarily spend the whole day with a client. Glenda does. She is not just a guide, she is a teacher. She teaches about the river and the fish, and gives you instruction on how to improve your cast.

Even experienced fly fishers sign up with Glenda for instruction on some of the fine points of the sport. She is in demand and must be booked far in advance. As a woman, it was not easy for her to gain this standing.

Glenda was raised in a suburb of Belfast, where her father was a policeman. A Belfast policeman is one of the toughest jobs imaginable. "I caught my first fish, an eel, when I was six," she told me. "My uncle Michael was a fly-tier. He never took me fishing, but I used to watch him tie. When I was twelve he died and left me his rods. I started fishing early before school, then after school, then when I should have been in school. My father, a policeman, did not approve. But half the school used to skip for the first day of the brown trout season. I asked if I could too and the teacher said yes and then for the next five years I skipped on opening day.

"When I was eighteen, I told my parents I was going to fish for the rest of my life and they nearly killed me. I deliberately flunked my police exam. I didn't want to be a policeman, I wanted to fish. I came from the North and the fishing wasn't very nice where we were. I went to Scotland to learn how to fish."

Even when Glenda became a skilled fisher, men would not listen to a word she had to say. She started giving casting demonstrations and, like Joan Wulff, soon realized that to get what she wanted, she had to become a champion caster. She had no more desire to do so than Joan had, but she entered competition after competition and became the women's world salmon long-distance casting champion. No one questioned her again. She never entered another casting competition again either.

Glenda and her husband, Noel, lease several beats of the Blackwater from its owner. As in Britain, Irish rivers have owners.

The Irish have learned the lessons of their hard history well. During what they call the Great Hunger, caused by a blight in the potato crop between 1845 and 1849, a million Irish died and at least that many immigrated. Ireland still contains nowhere near its 1844 population. But while the Irish peasants starved, the Irish landowners made handsome incomes by selling the plentiful food they produced, including huge quantities of salmon, to England. The great lesson learned was the importance of owning land—what Maurice Walsh called "the terrible Irish land hunger." So owning a river is a very important thing in Ireland and leasing out beats is profitable business.

According to Glenda and Noel, holding a lease on a beat is a demanding full-time job. But they don't complain. How many people get to earn their living fly fishing? They have exclusive rights to five miles of the Blackwater on which they support themselves and their two children, who have an idyllic childhood. "It's a tough life but it's about the quality of life, loving what you do," Glenda says. "People say they envy me, but most wouldn't want to live on what I earn. I am one of the few, maybe the only one in Ireland, who earns a living completely on guiding and teaching."

I had booked a few days to go fishing with Glenda. We were using a cascade, a modest-size salmon fly with an orange-and-yellow buck tail—dyed fur from a deer's tail—with a little silver and red and orange hackle made from chicken feathers. Tied on a double hook, it seemed to me a worthy fly, not overdone.

The salmon were less impressed. I saw a few big ones jump up to check me out, but since they were not feeding, my theory was that they were teasing me.

The river was also alive with leaping brown trout, who were eating. A thick swatch of little wispy black flies called olive flies were hovering above the river. Glenda had an artificial olive fly in her box, and we tried it, but the fish wouldn't take it.

Then we tried a silver spider, a fly designed to look like a minnow. Suddenly I was catching nice-sized salmon smolts, vigorous and ready for their adventure at sea. I also caught a large brown trout. Every river has its own brown trout, and in the Blackwater they are handsome, with speckled backs and golden bellies.

But this did not make us happy. The fish were all taking the silver spider, not the olive fly imitation. This meant that despite the trout leaping in the air, they were not eating insects. Both the trout and the salmon smolts were feeding on fry, which are baby salmon, and that is what they mistook the silver spider for. We wished they were eating flies.

Another morning on the Blackwater, I was catching absolutely nothing. There was not even a sign of a leaping fish. No one else on the river was catching anything either. At midday I decided to take a break and tie flies with Noel. Glenda announced that she knew a good spot and was going off by herself to catch a salmon. Noel taught me how to tie cascades. After a time, Glenda returned. She had caught nothing. Noel smiled, "Aye, Mark, you fished her to a draw!"

And that is it. There is the green stone-strewn countryside, the thick dark woods, and the way the charcoal clouds break up and allow brilliant rays of light to blaze through in the glens. And there is the humor of the people who love to laugh. When you are in Ireland, you will not always catch a fish, but you will always laugh.

TO BE HONEST, Yeats probably never fished the Blackwater. He was a West Country lad from Sligo and Mayo, and so more likely fished the River Moy. Later he lived in Dublin and in

London and didn't fish at all anymore, a sad fate for an Irishman. But he always looked back on his Sligo days, when, as he put it, "I was a boy with never a crack in my heart."

The freckled fly fisherman wearing wool clothes made in Connemara in Yeats's poem above is a simple man, but wise. He climbs the hilly riverbank at gray dawn and casts his flies. He always knows what is important and that life is not always about victory. The fish are there and he is always optimistic that at any moment one will rise and take his fly and he will have his moment. His hands are aching for that "delicious tug." His arm remembers.

The man in the gray Connemara clothes also knows that in the end, he doesn't win. The river wins and that is how it is supposed to be. Still, he can stand in the middle of a river's gurgling greatness and dare to hope. The Czech writer Ota Pavel said it best. "Finally, I have found the right word," he wrote. "Freedom. Fishing is freedom most of all."

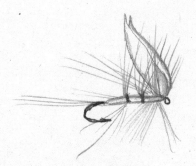

Ogden's fancy fly

ACKNOWLEDGMENTS

Thanks to Nancy Miller and the hard-working team at Bloomsbury, unstoppable even in a pandemic, and to my wonderful agent, Charlotte Sheedy, who is always unstoppable anyway, and to Talia and Marian, the best people to be locked up with.

APPENDIX: RIVERS IN THIS BOOK

Alta (Norway)
Ausable (New York)
Battenkill (Vermont)
Beaverkill (New York)
Big Blackfoot (Montana)
Big and Little Wood (Idaho)
Blackwater (Ireland)
Bonaventure (Quebec, Canada)
Boyd, tributary of Avon (England)
Brora (Scotland)
Chattahoochee (Georgia)
Clackamas (Oregon)
Columbia (Washington and Oregon)
Corrib (Ireland)
Dee (Scotland)
Deveron (Scotland)
Dove (Staffordshire, England)
Eel (California)
Eyak (Alaska)
Fraser (British Columbia, Canada)
Godbout (Quebec, Canada)
Grand and Petit Cascapédia (Quebec, Canada)
Irati (Navarra, Spain)
Itchen (Hampshire, England)
Kimobetsu (Hokkaido, Japan)
Kotui (Russia)
Laval (Labrador, Canada)
Lea (Hertfordshire, England)
Margaree (Nova Scotia, Canada)

Mashpee (Massachusetts)
McCloud (California)
Moisie (Labrador, Canada)
Moy (Ireland)
Namsen (Norway)
Ness (Scotland)
Neversink (New York)
Nipigon (Ontario, Canada)
Ozernaya (Kamchatka Peninsula, Russia)
Penobscot (Maine)
Restigouche (French Ristigouche; New Brunswick and
    Quebec, Canada)
Roaring Fork (Colorado)
Rogue (Oregon)
Salmon (Idaho)
Saloum (Senegal)
Schuylkill (Pennsylvania)
Shannon (Ireland)
Shirbetsu (Japan)
Silver Creek (Idaho)
Snake (Idaho and Wyoming)
Spey (Scotland)
Spruce Creek (Pennsylvania)
Stjørdal (Norway)
Suðurland (Iceland)
Tana (Norway)
Tay (Scotland)
Thurso (Scotland)
Trent (England)
Two Hearted River (Michigan)
Wandle (England)
Warm Springs Creek (Idaho)
Willamette (Oregon)
Yellow River (China and Tibet)

LIST OF ILLUSTRATIONS

BIBLIOGRAPHY

American Museum of Fly Fishing. *A Treasury of Reels: The Fishing Reel Collection*. Manchester, VT: American Museum of Fly Fishing, 1990.

Anderson, Dave, ed. *The Red Smith Reader*. New York: Skyhorse, 2014.

Barker, Thomas. *The Art of Angling: Wherein Are Discovered Many Rare Secrets, Very Necessary to Be Knowne by All That Delight in that Recreation*. London, 1651 (reprinted London: Inchbold and Gawtress, 1817).

Bei Dao. *City Gate, Open Up*. New York: New Directions, 2017. Originally published in 2010.

Bergman, Ray. *Trout*. Third Edition. New York: Alfred A. Knopf, 1976.

Berners, Juliana. *The Treatyse of Fysshynge wyth an Angle Attributed to Dame Juliana Berners*. London: John Pickering, 1827.

Bevan, Jonquil. *Isaak Walton's The Compleat Angler: The Art of Recreation*. New York: St. Martin's Press, 1988.

Blot, Pierre. *Hand-Book of Practical Cookery, for Ladies and Professional Cooks*. New York: Arno Press, 1973 (original 1869).

Bowen, Elizabeth. *Bowen's Court*. New York: Alfred A. Knopf, 1942.

Brautigan, Richard. *Trout Fishing in America*. New York: Delta, 1967.

Bryan, John, ed. *Fishing with Dad: 50 Great Writers Recall Angling with Their Fathers, Friends, and Favorite Colleagues*. New York: Skyhorse, 2012.

Butler, James E., and Arthur Taylor. *Penobscot River Renaissance: Restoring America's Premier Atlantic Salmon Fishery*. Camden, Maine: Silver Quill Press, 1992.

Carmichael, Hoagie B. *8*. North Salem, NY: Anesha, 2010.

———. *The Grand Cascapedia River: A History*. 2 vols. North Salem, NY: Anesha, 2012.

———. *Side Casts, A Collection of Fly fishing Yarns by a Guy Who Can Spin Them*. North Salem, NY: Anesha, 2015.

Carter, Jimmy. *An Outdoor Journal: Adventures and Reflections*. New York: Bantam Books, 1988.

Chouinard, Yvon, Craig Mathews, and Mauro Mazzo. *Simple Fly Fishing: Techniques for Tenkara and Rod and Reel*. Ventura, CA: Patagonia, 2014.

Cleland, Elizabeth. *A New and Easy Method of Cookery*. Facsimile of 1755 edition. Totnes, Devon, UK: Prospect Books, 2005.

Cleveland, Grover. *Fishing and Shooting Sketches*. New York: The Outing Press, 1906.

Combs, Trey. *Steelhead Trout: Life History, Early Angling, Contemporary Steelheading*. Portland, OR: Northwest Salmon Trout Steelheader Company, 1971.

Davy, Humphry. *Salmonia: or, Days of Fly Fishing*. London: John Murray, 1828.

Douglass, William A. *Casting About in the Reel World*. Oakland, CA: RDR Books, 2002.

Duncan, David James. *The River Why*. San Francisco: Sierra Club Books, 1983.

Dunham, Judith. *The Atlantic Salmon Fly: The Tyers and Their Art*. San Francisco: Chronicle, 1991.

Eckstorm, Fannie Hardy. *The Penobscot Man*. Boston: Houghton Mifflin, 1904.

Fagan, Brian. *Fishing: How the Sea Fed Civilization*. New Haven, CT: Yale University Press, 2017.

Fersen, Paul, and Margot Page. *The Art of Fly Fishing: An Illustrated History of Rods, Reels, and Favorite Flies*. Philadelphia: Courage, 2000.

Foggia, Lyla. *Reel Women: The World of Women Who Fish*. New York: Three Rivers Press, 1995.

Gao Xingjian. *Buying a Fishing Rod for My Grandfather: Stories*. New York: HarperCollins, 2004.

Garrison, Everett E., and Hoagy B. Carmichael. *A Master's Guide to Building A Bamboo Fly Rod: The Essential and Classic Principles and Methods*. North Salem, NY: Anesha, 2016.

Goodspeed, Charles Eliot. *Angling in America: Its Early History and Literature*. Boston: Houghton Mifflin, 1939.

Grey, Zane. *Tales of Fishes*. New York: Grosset & Dunlap, 1920.

———. *Tales of Freshwater Fishing*. New York: Grosset & Dunlap. 1928.

———. *Tales of Southern Rivers*. New York: Grosset & Dunlap, 1924.

Haig-Brown, Roderick. *The Seasons of a Fisherman: A Fly Fisher's Classic Evocations of Spring, Summer, Fall, and Winter Fishing*. New York: Lyons, 2000.

————. *Woods and River Tales*. Toronto: McClelland and Stewart, 1980.

Halverson, Anders. *An Entirely Synthetic Fish: How Rainbow Trout Beguiled America and Overran the World*. New Haven, CT: Yale University Press, 2010.

Harper, Francis, ed. *The Travels of William Bartram*. Athens, GA: University of Georgia Press, 1998.

Hemingway, Ernest. "Big Two-Hearted River, Part I and Part II." *The Complete Short Stories of Ernest Hemingway*. New York: Scribner's, 1987.

————. *The Sun Also Rises*. New York: Scribner's, 1926.

Hemingway, Jack. *Misadventures of a Fly Fisherman: My Life with and without Papa*. Dallas: Taylor, 1986.

Hoffman, Richard C. *Fishers' Craft and Lettered Art: Tracts on Fishing from the End of the Middle Ages*. Toronto: University of Toronto Press, 1997.

Holden, Dr. George Parker. *The Idyl of the Split-Bamboo: A Detailed Description of How to Build a Bamboo Fly fishing Rod*. Cincinnati: Stewart & Kidd, 1920.

Hoover, Herbert. *Fishing for Fun and to Wash Your Soul*. New York: Random House, 1963.

Irving, Washington. *Sketch Book of Geoffrey Crayon, Gent*. New York: C.S. Van Winkle, 1819.

Johnson, Kirk Wallace. *The Feather Thief: The Natural History Heist of the Century*. London: Windmill Books, 2014.

Johnson, Victor R., Jr. *America's Fishing Waders: The Evolution of Modern Fishing Waders*. Vallejo, CA: EP Press, 2008.

Jorgensen, Poul. *Dressing Flies for Fresh and Salt Water*. Rockville Center, NY: Freshet Press, 1973.

―――. *Salmon Flies: Their Character, Style, and Dressing*. Harrisburg: Stackpole, 1978.

Kelson, George M. *The Salmon Fly: How to Dress It and How to Use It*. London: Wyman and Sons, Ltd, 1895.

Latimer, Adrian. *Fire & Ice: Fly fishing through Iceland*. Ellesmere, Shropshire, UK: Medlar Press, 2012.

Leonard, J. Edson. *The Essential Fly Tier*. Englewood Cliffs, NJ: Prentice-Hall, 1976.

Leslie, Eliza. *Miss Leslie's Directions for Cookery: An Unabridged Reprint of the 1851 Classic*. Mineola, NY: Dover, 1999.

Lloyd, Captain L. *The Field Sports of the North of Europe: A Narrative of Angling, Hunting, and Shooting in Sweden and Norway*. London: Hamilton, Adams, 1885.

Lolli, Tony. *The Art of the Fishing Fly*. New York: Sterling, 2018.

Maclean, Norman. *A River Runs Through It*. Chicago: University of Chicago Press, 1976.

Marbury, Mary Orvis. *Favorite Flies and Their Histories*. Secaucus, NJ: Wellfleet, 1988 (original 1892).

Mascall, Leonard. *A Booke of Fishing with Hooke and Line*. London: John Wolfe, 1590.

Maunsell, G. W. *The Fisherman's Vade Mecum: A Compendium of Precepts, Counsel, Knowledge and Experience in Most Matters Pertaining to Fishing for Trout, Sea Trout, Salmon and Pike*. London: Adam & Charles Black, third edition, 1952.

May, Robert. *The Accomplisht Cook*. Facsimile of 1685 edition. Totnes, Devon, UK: Prospect, 1994.

McClintock, James. *A Naturalist Goes Fishing: Casting in Fragile Waters from the Gulf of Mexico to New Zealand's South Island.* New York: St. Martin's Press, 2015.

McDonald, John, ed. *The Complete Fly Fisherman: The Notes and Letters of Theodore Gordon.* London: Jonathan Cape, 1949.

———. *The Origins of Angling: An Inquiry into the Early History of Fly Fishing with a New Printing of The Treatise of Fishing with an Angle.* New York: Lyons & Burford, 1957.

McGuane, Thomas. *The Longest Silence: A Life in Fishing.* New York: Alfred A. Knopf, 1999.

McKenna, Mike. *Angling Around Sun Valley: A Year-round Fly Fishing Guide to South Central Idaho.* Hailey, ID: Mandala Media, 2013.

Mills, Derek, and Jimmy Younger. *Megan Boyd: The Story of a Salmon Flydresser.* Ludlow, Shropshire, UK: Merlin Unwin Books, 2016.

Netboy, Anthony. *The Atlantic Salmon: A Vanishing Species?* Boston: Houghton Mifflin, 1968.

Pavel, Ota. Translated by Jindriska Badal and Robert McDowell. *How I Came to Know Fish.* New York: New Directions, 1990.

Prosek, James. *The Complete Angler: A Connecticut Yankee Follows in the Footsteps of Walton.* New York: HarperCollins, 1999.

———. *Trout: An Illustrated History.* New York: Alfred A. Knopf, 1997.

Pryce-Tannatt, T. E. *How to Dress Salmon Flies.* London: Adam and Charles Black, 1977. First edition 1914.

Radcliffe, William. *Fishing from the Earliest Times.* Chicago: Ares, 1974. First published in London by John Murray, 1921.

Sage, Dean. *The Ristigouche and Its Salmon Fishing*. Edinburg: David Douglas, 1888.

Schullery, Paul. *American Fly Fishing*. Manchester, VT: American Museum of Fly Fishing, 1987.

———. *Royal Coachman: The Lore and Legends of Fly-Fishing*. New York: Simon & Schuster, 1999.

Scott, Genio C. *Fishing in American Waters*. Secaucus, NJ: Castle Books, 1989 (originally published in 1888).

Shand, Mel. *A Portrait of the River Dee*. Aboyne, Scotland: Pica Design, 2014.

Sheringham, Hugh, and John C. Moore, eds. *The Book of the Fly-Rod*. Lanham, MD: Derrydale Press, 1993.

Steinbeck, John. "On Fishing." *America and Americans and Selected Nonfiction*. Edited by Jackson J. Benson and Susan Shillinglaw. New York: Viking, 2002.

Taylor, Joseph E., III. *Making Salmon: An Environmental History of the Northwest Fisheries Crisis*. Seattle: University of Washington Press, 1999.

Thoreau, Henry D. *A Week on the Concord and Merrimack Rivers*. West Virginia Pulp and Paper Company, 1966. Originally published in Boston by James Monroe in 1849.

———. *The Maine Woods*. Princeton: Princeton University Press, 1972. Originally published posthumously in 1864.

Train, Arthur. *Mr. Tutt at His Best*. New York: Scribner's, 1961.

Trench, Charles Chenevix. *A History of Angling*. London: Hart-Davis, MacGibbon, 1974.

Walsh, Maurice. *Green Rushes*. London: W & R Chambers, 1936.

Walton, Isaak. *The Compleat Angler; or, the Contemplative Man's Recreation: Being a Discourse of Fish and Fishing for the Perusal of Anglers; with Instructions How to Angle for a Trout or Grayling in a Clear Stream, by Charles Cotton* [fifth edition, 1676] *and with an Introduction by James Russell Lowell.* New York: Heritage Press, 1948.

Waterman, Charles F. *A History of Angling.* Tulsa: Winchester Press, 1981.

Whitelaw, Ian. *The History of Fly Fishing in Fifty Flies.* New York: Abrams, 2015.

Wilkinson, A. G. "Notes on Salmon Fishing." *Scribner's Monthly* 12, no. 6. (October 1876).

Woit, Steve. *Fly Fishing Treasures: The World of Fly Fishers and Collecting.* London: Pureprint, 2018.

Wood, Charles B., III. *Bibliotheca Salmo Salar: A Selection of Rare Books, Manuscripts, Journals, Diaries, Photograph Albums, & Ephemera on the Subject of Atlantic Salmon Fishing.* Boston: David R. Godine, 2017.

Wulff, Joan Salvato. *Joan Wulff's Fly Fishing: Expert Advice from a Woman's Perspective.* Harrisburg: Stackpole, 1991.

Wulff, Lee. *Bush Pilot Angler.* Camden, ME: Down East Books, 2000.

———. *The Atlantic Salmon.* New York: A. S. Barnes, 1958.

Wulff, Lee. Edited by John Merwin. *Salmon on a Fly: The Essential Wisdom and Lore from a Lifetime of Salmon Fishing.* New York: Simon & Schuster, 1992.

INDEX

Note: page numbers in *italics* refer to illustrations.

A NOTE ON THE AUTHOR

MARK KURLANSKY is the *New York Times* bestselling author of *Milk!*, *Havana*, *Paper*, *The Big Oyster*, *1968*, *Salt*, *The Basque History of the World*, *Cod*, and *Salmon*, among other titles. He has received the Dayton Literary Peace Prize, *Bon Appétit's* Food Writer of the Year Award, the James Beard Award, and the Glenfiddich Award. He lives in New York City. www.markkurlansky.com